IN THIS SANCTUARY

IN THIS SANCTUARY

—

An Invitation to Worship the Savior

—

Twila Paris
with Robert Webber

CELEBRATION/KINGDOM OF GOD
Words & music by Twila Paris
©Copyright 1990 Ariose Music/ASCAP (a division of Star Song Communications) & Mountain Spring Music/ASCAP. Administered by Gaither Copyright Management. All rights reserved. Used by permission.

COME WORSHIP THE LORD
Words & music by Twila Paris
©Copyright 1991 Ariose Music/ASCAP (a division of Star Song Communications) and Mountain Spring Music/ASCAP. Administered by Gaither Copyright Management. All rights reserved. Used by permission.

EVERY HEART THAT IS BREAKING
Words & music by Twila Paris
©Copyright 1988 Ariose Music/ASCAP (a division of Star Song Communications) and Mountain Spring Music/ASCAP. Administered by Gaither Copyright Management. All rights reserved. Used by permission.

HE IS EXALTED
Words & music by Twila Paris
©Copyright 1985 StraightWay Music/ASCAP (a division of Star Song Communications) & Mountain Spring Music/ASCAP. Administered by Gaither Copyright Management. All rights reserved. Used by permission.

HOSANNA
Words & music by Twila Paris
©Copyright 1991 Ariose Music/ASCAP (a division of Star Song Communications) & Mountain Spring Music/ASCAP. Administered by Gaither Copyright Management. All rights reserved. Used by permission.

I AM READY
Words & music by Twila Paris
©Copyright 1991 Ariose Music/ASCAP (a division of Star Song Communications) & Mountain Spring Music/ASCAP. Administered by Gaither Copyright Management. All rights reserved. Used by permission.

I WILL WAIT
Words & music by Twila Paris
©Copyright 1990 Ariose Music/ASCAP (a division of Star Song Communications) & Mountain Spring Music/ASCAP. Administered by Gaither Copyright Management. All rights reserved. Used by permission.

LAMB OF GOD
Words & music by Twila Paris
©Copyright 1985 StraightWay Music/ASCAP (a division of Star Song Communications) & Mountain Spring Music/ASCAP. Administered by Gaither Copyright Management. All rights reserved. Used by permission.

LET THEM PRAISE
Words & music by Twila Paris
©Copyright 1991 Ariose Music/ASCAP (a division of Star Song Communications) & Mountain Spring Music/ASCAP. Administered by Gaither Copyright Management. All rights reserved. Used by permission.

PRINCE OF PEACE
Words & music by Twila Paris
©Copyright 1987 Ariose Music/ASCAP (a division of Star Song Communications) & Mountain Spring Music/ASCAP. Administered by Gaither Copyright Management. All rights reserved. Used by permission.

RUNNING TO THE RESCUE
Words & music by Twila Paris
©Copyright 1987 Ariose Music/ASCAP (a division of Star Song Communications) & Mountain Spring Music/ASCAP. Administered by Gaither Copyright Management. All rights reserved. Used by permission.

THRONE ROOM SUITE
Words & music by Twila Paris
©Copyright 1987 Ariose Music/ASCAP (a division of Star Song Communications) & Mountain Spring Music/ASCAP. Administered by Gaither Copyright Management. All rights reserved. Used by permission.

THE WARRIOR IS A CHILD
Words & music by Twila Paris
©Copyright 1984 Singspiration Music/ASCAP. All rights reserved. Used by permission of Benson Music Group, Inc., Nashville, TN.

WE BOW DOWN
Words & music by Twila Paris
©Copyright 1983 Singspiration Music/ASCAP. All rights reserved. Used by permission of The Benson Company, Nashville, TN.

WE WILL GLORIFY
Words & music by Twila Paris
©Copyright 1982 Singspiration Music/ASCAP. All rights reserved. Used by permission of The Benson Company, Nashville, TN.

WE SHALL ASSEMBLE/ IN THIS SANCTUARY
Words & music by Twila Paris
©Copyright 1991 Ariose Music/ASCAP (a division of Star Song Communications) & Mountain Spring Music/ASCAP. Administered by Gaither Copyright Management. All rights reserved. Used by permission.

Star Song Publishing Group, a division of Jubilee Communications, Inc.
2325 Crestmoor, Nashville, Tennessee 37215

First Printing, October 1993

ISBN # 1-56233-101-9

Printed in the United States of America

1 2 3 4 5 6 7 8 9 10 — 99 98 97 96 95 94 93

CONTENTS

INTRODUCTION

In This Sanctuary is a book about public worship written by two people who are first and foremost worshipers and secondly people who have been given gifts by God which they have returned to the church.

Twila has been given the gift of leading worship through her music. Her concerts are worship events. People don't come to a Twila Paris concert only to be entertained, but also to worship the Living God. As Twila gets herself out of the way in her singing, God is worshiped, and the people become caught up in praise. While Twila's concerts are full of energy and allow a time for foot stomping and hand clapping, they also allow time for a quiet restfulness in the manifest presence of God. In these concerts, God inhabits the sanctuary of the gathered people because the focus is not on a person singing, but on the God to whom the songs are directed.

On the other hand, Bob is a worship teacher. Bob is not an ordained minister, but a committed Christian layman who loves worship and exercises the gift of teaching. In addition to teaching theology at Wheaton College, Bob conducts worship seminars in pastors' conferences and local churches. These seminars address the biblical foundations, the historical development, and the contemporary styles of worship. These seminars not only teach the principles of worship, they address matters dealing with the planning of worship and seek to move people beyond their comfort zones, stretching them toward new ways of worship.

In these gifts both bring to the people who hear them and to the readers of this book the two sides of Christianity everyone desires— experience and understanding. Every Christian wants to experience God and know God. Both Twila and Bob believe that in and through worship both the experiencing and the knowing occur. The God who is present touches our lives and heals us, and as we go from worship and reflect on this experience, our relationship with God is deepened.

BACKGROUND

In This Sanctuary comes from the experience of two people with a long family history in the Christian faith. Both come from ministry families that have passed down the faith, and both are grateful for God's genetic goodness in their lives.

Twila's great-grandparents, who were ministers of the gospel, moved across the Southern plains in the early part of the twentieth century setting up tent meetings and brush-arbor churches. Her grandparents were also pastors who started churches in areas where none existed. As one church was planted and brought to the place of relative independence, they moved on to another place to repeat the process of building the church. Twila's dad is an ordained minister and for much of his ministry has worked with Youth with a Mission, working with people who carry the gospel all over the world.

Bob spent his early childhood in Africa where his parents were missionaries with the African Inland Mission. When his parents returned to America, his dad became the pastor of the Montgomeryville Baptist Church, a church located twenty-five miles west of Philadelphia, the city of brotherly love.

Because of their backgrounds, both believe that the impact of a Christian family on a young life is beyond measure. Families who honor God and whose values are shaped by the Christian story are certainly necessary for the passing down of the faith. So, both give thanks for their godly heritage.

EARLY CHILDHOOD

Childhood is a formative time for all, and Twila and Bob are no exception to this rule. Sometimes in childhood it is already possible to see a person's interests and talent expressed. For most parents these early actions may be cute, but once a child has grown to maturity, the adult may look back and remember with fondness and some curiosity early signs of the later adult.

Because Twila was brought up in a family employed in an itinerant ministry (she didn't live in a home with her own bedroom until she was seven), she was a "team" member as far back as she can remember. Her "team" job was to sing. Twila is the oldest of four children, and she began to "solo" sing in the team ministry by the time she was three. And she cut her first record called "Twila Paris, America's Little Sweetheart" at eight.

Bob was also given signs of his calling at an early age. One of the "fun" things he did in Africa as early as five years of age was to gather the natives for "worship" around his slide (standing on top of it) where he "preached" to the native workers on their break.

Both Twila and Bob thank their parents for supporting them in these early indications of their future lives and work. And they both think that children are considerably more aware of the significance of worship and ministry than most people recognize.

COMMITMENT TO UNITY IN THE BODY OF CHRIST

Both also share a broad view of the church and long to see the divisions in the body of Christ healed. Twila developed her inclusive view of the church in Youth with a Mission, an evangelically-based ministry that includes Christians from every tradition—mainline Protestant, Pentecostal, Catholic, Evangelical, and Charismatic. Twila has, from her youth and from the example set by her parents, always worshiped with people from various traditions and consequently has always loved the whole church.

Bob's story is similar, but with a different twist. He grew up in a very closed atmosphere where his parents regarded their Christian label to be the one true expression of the faith. But as he pursued his education in a fundamentalist university and then in an Episcopal, then Presbyterian, and finally, a Lutheran Seminary, his view of the church as all the people of God in every denomination and all over the world emerged as a basic conviction of his heart.

In recent years the phenomenon of worship renewal has spread to nearly every Christian denomination. Each generation has succeeded in breaking down many of the old walls that Christians built to keep other Christians out. And, thanks be to God, worship, which is the identity of the church, has been the great equalizer. We are all one at the foot of the cross, in the confession of the thief, and by the wounded side.

The breadth Twila and Bob bring to this book is an example of this oneness. While both are Evangelical Christians, Twila represents the Interdenominational/Praise and Worship roots where she worships with conviction and personal ownership. Bob is a committed worshiper in the Episcopal Church. But neither would say that you have to belong to this or that particular branch of the church. Both insist that the arms of God stretch wide enough to spread around the world and embrace every expression of God's Church.

WHAT EACH AUTHOR
BRINGS TO IN THIS SANCTUARY

At first someone may think it strange that two people representing the free church and the liturgical church, concert halls and classrooms, audio tapes and books should be brought together. But for Twila and Bob nothing could be more natural and more challenging.

For one thing, they greatly appreciate how God has gifted them in different ways. Furthermore, the diversity in worship traditions represented by them is not a matter of conflict or confusion, but a sign of what is happening all over the world in worship. No longer do Christians always assemble with people of their own kind. Now worship gatherings and events bring people from every tradition together. Consequently, the choices of music in worship have become considerably more eclectic, drawing from the experience of the whole church. And in free churches, worship leaders frequently draw from the prayer book even as many liturgical churches now incorporate praise music. Worship brings together experience and thought. To divide the two is a great mistake, a mistake which Twila and Bob think must be overcome.

The Challenge

Twila and Bob want to challenge you to bring together heart and mind, practice and theory. They desire to challenge you personally and the local church to worship more deeply.

The church is in the midst of a great transition in worship, a transition which could head worship into an oversimplified form or into a fullness of renewal.

For example, the view that worship is singing and music only is a view that fails to recognize the much broader biblical teaching that worship includes preaching, communion, benedictions, the offering, prayer, baptism, the cycle of the Christian year and much more.

The church needs to be challenged in its present comfort zones of worship. It needs to stretch to be open to the restoration of much of what the Holy Spirit has given us through the history of God's worshiping people.

We hope this book will encourage you, stimulate you, and inspire you. You will do more than pick up this book, read it, and say, "Nice book, a good read." You will want to become an inquiring, active, and reforming worshiper. You will call your pastor, the deacons, or elders of your church and say, "We've got to change" and "Here's a book that will provide us with a direction rooted solidly in the biblical tradition, aware of the way the church has worshiped through the centuries, and radically committed to contemporary relevance."

THE PLAN OF THE BOOK

The plan or outline of *In This Sanctuary* is very simple. There are two parts to the overall structure. Part I deals with general thinking about the subject of worship, and Part II asks you to think specifically about what we do in worship. Both of these sections are reflective in nature and not given to the specifics or the "how to" of worship. The book ends with a chapter on how worship nurtures our spirituality.

Each chapter is conveniently divided into three parts: the first part introduces a song written by Twila, together with her own comments that interpret how the song is related to worship. The second section provides a devotional teaching by Bob on the theme addressed in Twila's song. The third part pulls together a brief challenge to make the kinds of changes that will continue to make worship a powerful and meaningful part of the local church and the Christian life.

PART I

Thinking About Worship

Introduction

In the ancient church there is a Latin saying used frequently by
the church fathers: lex orandi; lex credendi est.
This phrase literally interpreted means the rule of prayer is the rule of faith.
This means that how we pray or worship is
the way we believe: worship shapes believing. How we worship is
therefore of the utmost importance.
Part I is a study of worship, but not an abstract study
as you will see. It studies worship to see what
the people who worship believe. As you read Part I you will see that
worship is rooted in the gospel. Worship is the
gospel in motion, the gospel proclaimed, enacted, remembered, and celebrated.
For example, the content of each chapter
unfolds the gospel and shows how the gospel is the heartbeat
of our worship. Note how the titles of each chapter capture gospel themes:
—2 —
We worship out of our brokenness
—3 —
Jesus restores our relationship to God
—4 —
Worship is the work of the church
—5 —
In worship we remember and give thanks
We begin in Chapter One with an attempt to clarify
the concept that worship enacts
the gospel, and in Chapters Two through Five we will delve
more deeply into the subject.

Chapter One

Lift Up Your Hearts

"When we gather to worship, we proclaim, enact, remember, and celebrate the story of God's redeeming love."

Come worship the Lord God Almighty
For His loving-kindness is everlasting
His mercy endureth forever
His mercy endureth forever
His mercy endureth forever and ever and ever
Come worship the Lord, Come worship the Lord
Come worship the Lord

("Come Worship the Lord")

INTERPRETATION

I wrote "Come Worship the Lord" to express my own personal commitment in life. Worship is the central focus of my life, and I want to tell you about my childhood so you can understand how worship became so significant to me.

I grew up as a preacher's kid, traveling in an itinerant ministry with my parents. I have been singing for as long as I can remember. My parents tell me that at age two and three I was already making up songs and singing them. I'm sure they were not very good songs, but it is interesting to me that God placed songs in my heart at such an early age. I don't say that with pride; I just want to acknowledge those songs and my songs now as a gift from the Lord.

Actually not only the songs but also the privilege to minister through music are **all** precious gifts from Him. I feel it's critically important for me to stay focused on what God has called me to do.

The specifics of God's priorities for this ministry first became clear to me in 1982. I had recently started my recording career. A young man named Jack Wright (who is now my husband) began attempting to schedule concerts for me. He would call a church and say, "Could Twila Paris sing three songs in your evening service?" and they would say, "Twila who?"

While Jack was trying to figure out what he could tell a pastor about me, my dad, an ever-present influence in my life, challenged me by saying, "Why don't you go and ask the Lord to help you describe what your vision, your purpose, and your calling is? Don't think of yourself as one more person writing songs, but ask, 'Lord, what's my ministry?'"

I did just that.

I went off alone to pray and to hear from the Lord. A few days later I knew that one of the things I was called to emphasize was "praise and worship." So that's who I am, that's what my songs are about, and that's the emphasis of this book.

"Come Worship the Lord" is one of those songs that came to me as a gift. I don't even remember the circumstances of its origin as a song. Of course, the words are right from the Scripture. The Scripture was in my heart, and I was working around the house or sitting at the piano when the song came to me. I don't mean to sound mystical. But I do believe that when the Word of God is in your heart, whether you have learned it at home or in the church or in private meditation, it will often burst forth in words of praise. That's been my experience, and that's where "Come Worship the Lord" came from.

The song is obviously an invitation to worship. It encourages us to respond to God because God's "loving kindness is everlasting, His mercy endureth forever." Of course, that is what the heart of worship is all about—responding to God who is so good to us. By "good" I don't mean that God gives us all the things we want. That's a false and superficial concept of God. God is good to us in that God has freed us from the power of the evil one through Jesus Christ and has given us the discipline to choose to live in obedience to His will. So, whether we are going through times of trial or times of great happiness, God's loving-kindness and goodness are like a steady hand in our lives. So, in everything we are to give thanks and worship the Lord.

I not only love to worship, I love to watch people who are worshiping. The psalmist says, "It is fitting for the upright to praise him" (Ps. 33:1). I read that verse one day, and as I meditated on it, it struck me with its truth. Sometimes when I'm in a group of people who are worshiping, particularly if they are singing with their eyes closed and their hands raised, I'll take a peek at them. And I'm always impressed by how beautiful they look. People seem to glow and radiate when they worship.

I remember my grandmother used to say to me, "Oh Twila, blue is so becoming on you." She meant that I look good in blue. This idea also pertains to worship. Praise is becoming to the upright. When we worship, praise produces a radiant beauty on our faces because of our contact with God.

More important, in worship we are especially beautiful to God. Worship is a sweet aroma to God. For me, the fact that God loves our worship is a very challenging and motivating truth, a truth that I stress in all my worship songs. In my song, "This Celebration," I have tried to capture how our worship is pleasing to God. The song names who God is and praises God for God's person. Of course, this is what we do when we gather together to worship: we lift up our hearts in response to God.

> *Shout for joy unto the Lord of Hosts*
> *Celebrate His holiness, celebrate His power*
> *Shout for joy unto the Lord of Hosts*
> *Celebrate His mercy, celebrate His love*
> *Unto the King, this celebration*
> *Unto the King*

Unto the King
Unto the King, this celebration
Unto the King
Unto the King

("THIS CELEBRATION")

DEVOTIONAL TEACHING

Most of us really want to do what Twila encourages us to do in her song, "Come Worship the Lord." We want to worship. We don't want to play at worship, pretend to worship, or merely go through the motions.

But my impression is that many people go to worship in a very thoughtless manner, not thinking about what it is that they are about to do. So they enter into the community of worship with very little sense of what worship is all about. I know I've gone to worship thoughtlessly on many occasions.

For example, back in 1968 when I was a member of a conservative Presbyterian Church, I was generally unaware of the meaning and even the significance of worship. I went along with the crowd, went through the motions, paid my dues, chatted with a lot of people, and went home. It was a great social event, and I always enjoyed being among the people of God and my friends.

But one Sunday the pastor announced that he was going to teach a series of classes on worship. I thought, "Well, that's nice, I don't really know much about the subject, so it will be interesting to learn about it." Frankly, I don't remember anything that was said. My guess is that it wasn't particularly challenging or thoughtful. But I do remember my feelings and my response to the talks. Because the talks were superficial, I thought "is that all there is?" However, because the talks were lacking in content, I was driven to find out more about worship.

At first I began to be critical of worship. As I reflected on the subject, it occurred to me that a lot of worship was far too intellectual. Sometimes I felt that I had simply walked out of my classroom at Wheaton College and walked into a classroom in a church that added a few songs and took an offering. The more I thought about it, the more it didn't sit right with me. "Is worship primarily teaching?" I asked myself. My heart and my head said no, but I didn't have any other model as an alternative. So I went along with it, but continued to grow in my uneasiness.

I began to visit a few other churches to taste their worship in hopes I would find a worship that would fill my empty soul. In some churches I found just the opposite of my home church. These were the churches that were charged with emotion. I loved the fact that they preached the gospel, but every Sunday the sermon was a variation on the same theme. And the service always ended with an invitation to receive Jesus or rededicate your life. While I was glad that people came forward to receive Jesus, I still felt I hadn't worshiped. It seemed to me that this wasn't worship, but evangelism. It was like a Sunday morning crusade, week after week. "Worship has got to be something different from evangelism," I thought to myself.

I dubbed these two approaches to worship "classroom worship" and "tent worship." Those "cute" terms didn't mean that I dismissed teaching or evangelism as unnecessary. Obviously the church must teach and the church must evangelize. But when does it worship? What is worship?

Just about the time I thought I was starting to understand this elusive practice called worship, a new form emerged which I and many others have dubbed "entertainment worship." This approach, fueled by the media phenomena of the twentieth century, is, in many cases, a carbon copy of pop culture. In this new form of worship, music is the new sacrament. Churches have even shifted from being preacher-driven to being music-driven. Years ago people would look for a church with a good preacher. While many churches are still preacher-driven, the shift is decidedly toward a music-driven church. Church shoppers and consumers want a good "music program." If it's not there, a worship shopper is most likely to continue the search.

Almost anyone can identify with these three approaches to worship. If you have ever gone home from worship saying, "That was too intellectual" or "That was too emotional" or "I think that was a little heavy on the entertainment side," then you not only know what I'm writing about, you have experienced it. You haven't felt that your need to worship was satisfied.

BIBLICAL AUTHORITY

So how do we define worship? The most obvious place for us to start is with the Scripture. Christians have always confessed that the Scripture is the authoritative source of truth. If you want to know something about God or about the human condition or about salvation, you turn to the Bible. I hope you agree with me that the same principle of biblical authority should rule in questions about worship.

Actually it may seem strange that I need to make an assertion of biblical authority concerning worship. However, I often speak about my concern for a biblically-driven worship at pastors' conferences, and everyone nods and says, "Yes, yes, that's right, Bob, I agree." But then, many go back to their local churches and continue an "as always worship" or search for a worship that gains instant popular response.

What's popular today is a market-driven worship. The most prominent question I hear many church leaders asking is not "What does God have to say about worship?" but "What do the people want?" I really don't think these two questions need to be mutually exclusive. Both questions should be asked, but the first has to be the basis for worship.

BIBLICAL WORSHIP

To answer the question "What does the Bible have to say about worship?" thoroughly, we would have to walk through the entire Bible from Genesis through Revelation. That's because the entire Bible is the book of Christian worship. We all acknowledge the place of the Bible in worship when we read and preach from the Scriptures or when we sing a biblical refrain or when we challenge the church with the Scripture.

Imagine for a moment that you attended a worship where the worship leader admonished you with pithy sayings from Augustine, Thomas Aquinas, Martin Luther, John Calvin, or John Wesley. And then, when it came time for the Bible reading, a passage from one of C.S. Lewis' many writings was read. While each of these persons may have Christian insights into life, insights that are inspiring and noble, you would have every right to stand up and stomp out of the church. Why? Their writings are not in the worship book of the church—the Bible. They may comment on the church's worship book, but they are not the real thing. Each of us knows instinctively that the Bible is the book of Christian worship.

But once we acknowledge the Bible as the book of worship, we need to get inside its covers to find out what it says about worship. For one thing the Scripture contains numerous expressions of worship. What comes to mind immediately is the book of Psalms or the great heavenly hymns found in the book of Revelation. The Scripture also speaks about institutions of worship. For example, the Old Testament is filled with information about the worship of the Tabernacle and the Temple. And the New Testament, while it does not have elaborate descriptions of worship like the Old Testament does, takes us into the heart of the church as it worships, into its singing, baptism, preaching, and communion. In addition, the Scriptures contain instructions about worship. For example, the book of Exodus provides elaborate instruction on how to build the Tabernacle while the book of Leviticus lays down the rules for the sacrifices in great detail. And then there is the book of Hebrews, a writing that shows how all the worship of the Old Testament is fulfilled in Jesus our High Priest.

Obviously, space does not allow us the luxury of examining all that the Bible says about worship. So I will go to the center of the issue and look at the heartbeat of worship as presented in Scripture. The heartbeat of biblical worship has to do with what God does; it has to do with God's saving events.

The Heartbeat of Biblical Worship

If you look at the story of the entire Bible from beginning to end, you will note that it revolves around events—the act of Creation, the Event of the Fall, the Exodus Event, the Christ Event, and the Event of the Second Coming. This is the structure of the Bible, the story line, you might say, around which everything in the Scriptures revolves. This story line is not only the story line of the Bible; it is also the story line of worship since the Bible is the worship book of the church.

Let me give you one example of how this story line works in worship. I'll give more examples as this book unfolds, but for now this one example will help us get to the heart of worship.

I was visiting an evangelical church in the Wheaton area where I live, and the associate pastor prayed a prayer that I will never forget. After an opening hymn he said, "Let us pray," and these are the words that came out of his mouth:

"Lord, we bless You for creating us in Your image. And we thank You that after we fell away from You in sin, You did not leave us in our sin, but You came to us in Jesus Christ who lived among us, died for us, was buried and rose again, and ascended into heaven. And now, O Lord, as we await His coming again, receive our worship in His name."

When he prayed those words I said, "that's it, that's it." I wanted to leap on the pew in front of me and do a dance because he struck right at the heart of what we do in worship.

When we gather to worship, we proclaim, enact, remember, and celebrate the story of God's redeeming love. Twila captures this theme in her song "Come Worship the Lord" when she connects our worship with God's loving-kindness and mercy. If it had not been for God's loving-kindness and mercy, there would be no story to tell, to remember, to celebrate. But God did not leave us in our sins. God rescued us, and worship celebrates the rescue, the saving event.

In order to clarify this "event orientation" of worship, I'm going to ask you to think about the two central events of the Scripture — the Exodus Event and the Christ Event.

Suppose you walk up to a religious Jew and you ask that person, "What is the most important event in your history? What shapes and molds your life more than any other event?" A religious Jew will say, "The Exodus Event."

Why? A religious Jew will say something like this:

"Because in that event God rescued us from the clutches of Pharaoh, brought us up out of Egypt to Mt. Sinai, entered into covenant with us, and we became God's people, and God became our God."

Space does not permit me to develop the relationship of the Exodus Event to worship, but a study of Hebrew worship will show that the Exodus Event shaped all of its worship. For example, consider the nature of the Passover. The yearly celebration of the Passover proclaims, enacts, remembers, and celebrates God's saving actions in the Exodus Event.

Now let's move into the New Testament and ask a Christian, "What is the most important event in human history?" A Christian will answer, "The Christ Event, the living, dying, and rising of Christ."

Why? The Christian will say:

"Because in that event God in Christ brought us up out of our bondage to the powers of evil, entered into covenant with us, established the church, and we became God's people, and God became our God."

What stands at the very center of Israelite faith and Christian faith is God's saving event. And this saving event is the very heartbeat of worship.

The Scripture that focuses on the event orientation of faith and worship is found in Peter's epistle to the dispersed Christians who were suffering under the persecution of Nero. I can imagine that at a time when Christian leaders were being put to death, families were being destroyed, and people were fearing for their lives, they were asking some fundamental questions about themselves as the new people called "the church." Here are the words of Peter written to them in the midst of their trials:

"You are a chosen people, a royal priesthood, a holy nation, a people belonging to God, that you may declare the praises of him who called you out of darkness into his wonderful light. Once you were not a people, but now you are the people of God; once you had not received mercy, but now you have received mercy" (1 Pet. 2:9-10).

The point is that God's people are always a people of the event. The Hebrew people are people of the Exodus Event, and Christians are people of the Christ Event. And Peter goes right to the heart of worship when he says that we are to "declare the praises of him who called you out of darkness into his wonderful light."

Worship then is not primarily about me or my experience, but about God and God's saving action. Here is where we start with worship. But this starting point does not exclude me and my experience because there are two sides to worship. The one side is the divine action; the other is the human response. In worship God does what God has done in history. God continues to reach out to us, to bring us out of our bondage, to bring us through the Red Sea, to gather us at the mountain, to call us around the throne, to enter into covenantal relationship with us, to bring us healing, and to guide us toward the Promised Land.

Our response is to praise, to magnify, to lift up God and give God thanks. Twila captures this side of worship in her songs "We Will Glorify," "He Is Exalted," "Praise Him," "Let Them Praise," and "We Bow Down." This is the response that God wants, the response recorded in the life of Abraham, the patriarchs, Israel, the prophets, the primitive church, the church throughout the centuries, and the renewal of the twentieth century. And this is what God wants us to do in worship: remember His saving deeds and give thanks.

CHALLENGE

In this brief chapter we have attempted to define a biblical understanding of worship. We realize that the subject is more complicated than our presentation because the mystery of worship, like the mystery of God, is unfathomable. But we think it's faithful to the heart of Scripture to say that worship is first and foremost the proclamation, enactment, remembrance, and celebration of God's saving deeds. And that secondly, worship is the response of the people who praise, exalt, and extol the God of their salvation as they remember God's saving deeds.

In worship the church enacts the story which gives meaning to its existence and shape to its presence in the world. Therefore, the challenge that lies before us is one of forming a worship that is faithful to its biblical foundation. God wants us to be the people of the Christ Event. God wants the pattern of the death and resurrection which we remember in worship to shape us individually and collectively. God wants us to continually die to the power of sin and continually be raised to a new life in the Spirit. In God's worship, worship not only remembers that pattern of the life, death, and resurrection of Jesus, but forms the pattern of our spirituality after the pattern of His life, death, and resurrection. In worship we not only remember God's saving deeds with thanksgiving, we are shaped by God's deeds into the people of Christ, the people of the event.

In the next chapter, "We Worship Out of Our Brokenness," we will see how our sinful condition necessitated the saving event, the event which we continually celebrate in worship.

CHAPTER TWO

We Worship Out of Our Brokenness

"When we come to God acknowledging our sin, we can experience the healing offered by God through Jesus Christ for the sins of the whole world and we can return to God our offering of praise and thanksgiving."

Search my heart, make me clean
It's Your approval I long for
Rule my life, be my King
Do what You will
I belong to You

I will find my hope in You
Trusting in no man
Leaning not to earthly wisdom
Things I understand

Hide my heart away
Fill me with Your mind
Let the world forsake me
I will find my hope in You

Lord of my heart
Lord of my heart
I offer praise
From the shadow of Your throne
Lord of my heart
Lord of my heart
One song I raise in Your presence
You alone are Lord

Lord of the earth
Lord of the earth
We offer praise
From the shadow of Your throne
Lord of the earth
Lord of the earth
One song we raise in Your presence
You alone are Lord

("Throne Room Suite")

INTERPRETATION

I was raised in a Christian home where God was honored. Our home was filled with prayer, and God was spoken about as if He was an ever-present member of our family. I knew at an early age that I needed God; I needed to know Him personally. So I committed myself to Him at the age of four.

While I consider my conversion at an early age to be valid, I certainly didn't understand everything at that time about what I was doing. I just wanted to show Jesus that I loved Him. I wanted to be His child. Jesus urges the little children to come to Him, and so I did.

As I grew up, I became aware of my own sin and the sin of the world, even though I lived a rather protected life. I began to understand that I needed healing that only Jesus can give. I learned that the Scriptures teach that we can't truly worship God until we come to God out of a sense of our need. This is the great truth I wanted to express in "Throne Room Suite."

The song begins with the words "search my heart, make me clean." When God searches the hearts of even His children He sometimes finds them filled with rebellion and selfishness and in need of His cleansing. The Scriptures are clear that all of us have sinned and turned against God. As Paul states, "All have turned away, they have together become worthless; there is no one who does good, not even one" (Rom. 3:12).

A broader awareness of the sinful condition of people in general is expressed in another song "Prince of Peace." Here I see a world that denies God and believes a lie, minds that analyze God and choose death, a world full of fear, and godless nations that choose to go their own way. This is a world that has no peace and has not found its home. This is a world that needs to turn from its sinful rebellion and allow God to set His feet on the mountaintop again and take His throne:

There is no hope for a world that denies You
Firmly believing a lie
Hiding the hearts while the minds analyze You
Cleverly choosing to die
Maker of all, we kneel interceding
Fighting for Your will
Father of life, Your children are pleading still

Prince of Peace, come and reign
Set Your feet on the mountaintop again
Take Your throne, rightful Lord
Prince of Peace, come and reign forevermore

There is no peace for a new generation
Living and growing in fear
There is no home in a godless nation
Take Your authority here
Maker of all, we kneel interceding
Fighting for Your will
Father of life, Your children are pleading still

Prince of Peace, come and reign
Set Your feet on the mountaintop again
Take Your throne, rightful Lord
Prince of Peace, come and reign forevermore

Thy Kingdom come, Thy will be done
Thy Kingdom come, Thy will be done

Prince of Peace, come and reign
Set Your feet on the mountaintop again
Take Your throne, rightful Lord
Prince of Peace, come and reign forevermore
Prince of Peace, come and reign forevermore

("Prince of Peace")

DEVOTIONAL TEACHING

In "Throne Room Suite" Twila has identified a fundamental part of biblical worship: we are incapable of worship because we are bound in our sins and unable to break out of our human condition. Just as Israel was in bondage to Pharaoh and stuck in that situation, unable to free itself from the yoke, so also all of humanity is in the tightened grip of the evil one, totally unable to extricate itself.

If we are really to understand worship, we need to grasp how all of us are imprisoned by the powers of evil. For example, a number of years ago Karl Menninger, a well-known psychiatrist, authored a book entitled, What Ever Happened to Sin. The book was an instant best-seller, not only among religious people, but in the secular market as well. He had identified the reality of the great cover-up. While society was increasing in violence, hate, greed, lust, and in what the Bible calls the sins of the flesh, society was at the same time rationalizing its own evil in psychological jargon that sidestepped the real problem—sin. Ultimately sin is a breakdown of our relationship to God, and that breakdown manifests itself in the world as violence, hate, greed, etc. Before we can worship, we must re-establish our relationship to God.

I want to analyze this matter of sin and to search out how an acknowledgment of our sinful condition is a necessary prerequisite to biblical worship. Since our worship arises out of God's redemptive activity, we need to have a clear sense of the extent of our sin and of the deep trouble in which we and all of humanity lie.

Through the Cross, God saves us out of our sin, and our worship is a response to God's saving activity. I grew up with a sense of sin, but I don't think I understood how desperate my condition, and that of the whole world, really was until I became aware of the fourfold extent of the fall: a broken relationship with God, in the inner self, with neighbor, and with nature.

A BROKEN RELATIONSHIP WITH GOD

The first and most severe result of sin is a broken relationship with God, a rupture that can be traced back to our first parents Adam and Eve (see Rom. 5:12).

Paul says the result of "going our own way" has resulted in "every kind of wickedness, evil, greed and depravity." We are "full of envy, murder, strife, deceit and malice." We are "gossips, slanderers, God-haters, insolent, arrogant and boastful." We "invent ways of doing evil." We "disobey parents"; we are "senseless, faithless, heartless, ruthless" (Rom. 1:29-31).

The point Paul is making is that the break with God by Adam set in motion a chain of events in the life of the world that has affected us in every area of our lives. We have distorted and defaced the image in which we were created, and thus our relationship with God is broken. Instead of becoming "God-bearers," we have ended up bearing the image of the evil one.

A BROKEN INNER SELF

I'm not sure when I began to understand how deeply sin affects the inner person. Like most other people I took the divided, warring parts of my inner self as normal until I became more conscious of the restlessness in my inner person.

I identified with Cain. After Cain killed his brother Abel, God declared, ". . . you will be a restless wanderer on the earth" (Gen. 4:12). A vagrant and a wanderer is someone who is not only separated from something or someone external to himself, but one who is also alienated from himself. When Cain "went out from the Lord's presence" (Gen. 4:16), he began a long search for meaning.

The biblical record suggests that he sought meaning by building a city and by having a son. But the story of Cain is one of a man whose life is characterized by restlessness, wandering, and searching. As French educator and Christian philosopher Jaques Ellul suggests, "It is God's absence which is the never-ending sting planted in his heart . . . the search for home, the search for Eden, is in the end a constant desire for God's presence" (*The Meaning of the City,* 14).

Like Cain, all of us are aware of the loss of the presence of God and, therefore, of our own incompleteness. We do not know the true meaning of our lives, so we cast about for something or someone to give us personal meaning and security.

We are made by God and for God. The refusal to accept this relationship leads us into making a god of ourselves or some other aspect of the created order.

Because we turn to self in an autonomous way, we do not truly understand ourselves or the importance of a relationship with the Creator, a relationship that defines the meaning of our person and clarifies our function in the world. Instead, we elevate ourselves and become narcisstic and selfish. Orienting our life toward self-interest, whether through pleasure, power, sex, wealth, or any other number of self-oriented pursuits, we cut ourselves off from our true self.

Consequently, a breakdown occurs in our inner person, and a true assessment of our person cannot be made. The meaning of our existence and work has been severed from true understanding. We find a substitute in the elevation of self and in the finite realities of life at hand. But they are substitutes that do not answer our deepest needs, for until we know God, we do not know the true meaning of life in this world. Augustine, the renowned church father of the fifth century put it well: "Thou madest us for thyself, and our heart is restless until it reposes in thee" (*Confessions*, Book 1).

A Broken Relationship with Our Neighbor

As far back as I can remember, I considered fights and broken relationships with playmates and friends to be normal. It was not until I began to mature and to think about my situation in the world that I first began to observe how the broken relationships of the entire world are a global extension of the broken relationships I experienced in my own life.

I began to realize how we create the tone of our culture. Consequently, our culture reveals what we are as individuals, and we are alienated from our true self, which is God-centered. I saw how our personal departure from God influences the way we as members of society act toward each other. Because we have wandered from God, we create societies where people do not relate to each other positively.

This is the spiritual meaning of the Flood. The alienation from God that was first experienced by Adam and then passed down to succeeding generations resulted in a society that was described in the following terms: "The Lord saw how great man's wickedness on the earth had become, and that every inclination of the thoughts of his heart was only evil all the time" (Gen. 6:5).

Consequently, sin creates a destructive movement, a dynamic force that separates not only persons, but whole societies, even the whole of humanity, from the original meaning and purpose of life—communion with God.

Sin has unleashed the demonic powers that Paul labeled "rulers," "the authorities," "the powers of this dark world" and "spiritual forces of evil in the heavenly realms" (Eph. 6:12).

These powers seek to persuade us that we are, after all, autonomous. We do not need God. We can build our own lives without God. This attitude of independence lies at the heart of the ancient story of the tower of Babel. The theme of this event is not "reaching God" but building a monument to the glory and independence of man. "Come, let us build ourselves a city, with a tower that reaches to the heavens, so that we may make a name for ourselves and not be scattered over the face of the whole earth" (Gen. 11:4). These people thought they could master the powers of nature and be free from the authority of God. But the confusion of language that halted the project to promote their self-glory demonstrated the power of God over all attempts to create a meaningful world without God.

The history of the world points to repeated attempts of nations to create unity, establish peace, and live as brothers and sisters. While these efforts do sometimes result in short-term successes, they all ultimately go the way of the tower of Babel. The truth is that we cannot by ourselves break down the historical, cultural, and political barriers that stand in the way of being in communion with each other. It takes an act of God to do it.

A Broken Relationship with Nature

I think the recent "environmental crisis" has made me considerably more conscious of the biblical notion that even nature suffers as a result of the Fall (see Gen. 3:17-20). Creation was made to show forth God's glory. As the psalmist says, "The heavens declare the glory of God; the skies proclaim the work of his hands" (Ps. 19:1). But, because of the fall, creation itself is under "bondage to decay" (Rom. 8:21).

Perhaps the problems we are experiencing today with the breakdown of the ozone layer, the pollution of air and water, the so-called "greening effect," and the violence that is done to the earth through technological advances are all examples of how we have alienated ourselves from nature. To use a biblical idea, we have been "driven from the ground" (Gen. 4:11).

In the curse against Cain, God said, "Now you are under a curse and driven from the ground . . ." (Gen. 4:11); Cain, in response to God said, "Today you are driving me from the land . . ." (Gen. 4:14). These Scriptures have generally been recognized, especially by the Eastern church fathers, as statements that refer to the suffering of nature as a result of the Fall.

God had initially intended to communicate Himself through nature. Nature was to speak clearly and forcibly of God's special relationship with it. Although God can still speak through nature, the clarity of God's presence has been obscured. Because man the "microcosm" was given control over nature, our choice to serve Satan rather than God opened the creation up to the service of the evil one. Creation does not belong to Satan, but it has become the arena in which he exercises his influence over us. In this sense nature is alienated from God, even as we are alienated from God and from nature.

Implication of Sin for Worship

As I began to understand this four-fold extent of sin, I began to realize how utterly impossible it is for me, a participant in this sinful condition, to approach God in worship. Here is the scenario: because we have turned from God, distorted ourselves, set off a chain of cosmic broken relationships, and damaged the nature of social relationships, we have created a society full of conflict. Our rebellion against God has resulted in a culture in which relationships within marriage, the family, work, and all of society are in disarray. The whole world is in a bad situation, a state of sin. And no one is exempt. Each of us participates in the human condition of sinfulness. And in this condition we cannot worship God.

CHALLENGE

The first challenge that lies before us as worshipers is to recognize that we come to worship out of our sin and the brokenness of our relationship with God, with self, neighbor, and nature. Any other approach to the Holy, transcendent God who is above us and beyond us, the God whom we have offended by our rebellion, is an approach characterized by arrogance, haughtiness, pride, and a spirit of self-conceit.

Because of our sin, we do not have the ability to approach God in worship on our own. We can only come to God in Jesus Christ, who brings healing to all broken relationships. But when we come in Jesus' name, we bring with us the brokenness of the world. We bring our neighbor's anger, our city's violence, the world's estrangement, the crisis in nature. And when we come in the name of Jesus, the Son of God, we enter the presence of God through Jesus' stripes, received for us and for the whole world.

The point is that when we come to God acknowledging our sin, we can experience the healing offered by God through Jesus Christ for the sins of the whole world and we can return to God our offering of praise and thanksgiving.

A second challenge for us is to remember that the world can't worship and doesn't want to worship. So the church repents for the world, a world that doesn't know how to speak for itself.

Consequently, when we come to worship, we are to bring with us the sin of the whole world, all broken relationships with God, our broken selves, and the strife between peoples, nations, and nature.

The worship we offer to the Father is the work of Jesus. Only Jesus can repair our relationship to God; only Jesus can restore the relationships of neighbors who are torn with strife; only Jesus can bring healing to the nations; only Jesus can renew and restore the created order. Therefore, only Jesus is the true worship. Our worship is to remember and to give thanks in Jesus' name. And it is this subject, the significance of Jesus for our worship, which is the concern of the next chapter.

Chapter Three

Jesus Restores Our Relationship to God
"To worship means to declare that Jesus is Lord and Savior."

Running to the rescue
He will come to save you
Running to the rescue
He will come to save you

Listening every time you cry
He delights in you
Scattering evil left and right
Just to get you through

Running to the rescue
He will come to save you
Righteous anger flaming
Little child reclaiming

He is a Father to His own
Ever watching you
Said, "You will never be alone"
Every word is true

Call to the Lord who is worthy of praise
You will be saved from the enemy
He is your Shield and Salvation always
You will be saved from the enemy

Running to the rescue
He will come to save you
Righteous anger burning
Victory returning

Can you see Him coming?
See your Father running

Running to the rescue
He will come to save you
Running to the rescue
He will come to save you
Running to the rescue
He will come to save you
Running to the rescue
He will come to save you

("RUNNING TO THE RESCUE," PSALM 18:1-19)

INTERPRETATION

I've never thought of "Running to the Rescue" as a worship song, but it does have within it a theme that is very central to worship: God will come to save you! You can count on it!

I am unable to save myself. No matter how many songs I write, no matter how successful my career is, I can't save myself. I need the Cross and Resurrection, I need Christ to save me. I also need the Cross and Resurrection to be able to worship because without them I am trapped in my brokenness. So are you. But when God comes to save us, we are relocated in God and now able to respond in worship. This is what "Running to the Rescue" is about.

"Running to the Rescue" expresses the message of so many of the Psalms. For example, in Psalm 40 the psalmist is in a deep depression. Then God comes to rescue him, and the psalmist bursts forth with praise. "He lifted me out of the slimy pit, out of the mud and mire; he set my feet on a rock and gave me a firm place to stand. He put a new song in my mouth, a hymn of praise to our God" (Ps. 40:2-3). I think the movement of this psalm is so significant. Notice that first he was in despair (dislocated), then God brought him out of the mud and mire (relocated), and finally there was a new song in his mouth (worship).

This movement happens over and over again in life. It doesn't mean that a person gets saved again and again, but that the pattern of being in distress, being brought out, and praising God is not only the pattern of salvation, it is the pattern of the Christian life.

"Running to the Rescue" came out of this kind of situation in my life. The song came to me on one of those days when I felt overwhelmed with the circumstances of my life. And then I began to read Psalm 18, a psalm which demonstrates God's deliverance.

Here I saw David in anguish, crying out "the cords of death entangled me; the torrents of destruction overwhelmed me. The cords of the grave coiled around me; the snares of death confronted me" (Ps. 18:4-5).

"Well," I thought, "you can't get any more graphic than that, and that's exactly how I feel." As I read on, David said, "In my distress I called to the Lord; I cried to my God for help" (vs. 6). After this feeling of utter depression, David wrote the words of hope that are the theme of "Running to the Rescue": "From his temple he heard my voice" (vs. 6). And then finally, I was struck by the theme of God hearing and running to the rescue. Here is this person, David, or me, or anyone in distress. David calls out to the Lord. Or, I call out to the Lord, and what happens? The earth trembles and quakes, and the foundations of the mountains shake. Smoke comes out of the nostrils of God, consuming fire from His mouth, burning coals. God parts the heavens and comes down. He mounts the cherubim and flies. He soars on the wings of the wind and makes darkness His covering. The sky is full of hailstones and bolts of lightening. Arrows are flying everywhere. The enemies are scattered. Then God reaches down from on high, takes hold of David, pulls him out of deep waters and rescues him (see verses 7-19).

I love the drama of Psalm 18 because the word pictures of that psalm describe the extent to which God will go to come to my rescue, to your rescue. God's work of salvation is full of dramatic action and life.

As a matter of fact, I like to think of worship as a great drama. Here we are, captured by sin, in prison to the evil one, with no hope of release. But God comes to the rescue.

My own personal response when I think of how God comes to release us and save us is best expressed in "He Is Exalted." I want to praise and exalt Him forever, to claim Him as Lord, to recognize that God's truth will reign forever, and that His holy name will forever be exalted on high:

> *He is exalted, the King is exalted on high*
> *I will praise Him*
> *He is exalted, forever exalted, and I will praise His name*
> *He is the Lord*
> *Forever His truth shall reign*
> *Heaven and earth rejoice in His holy name*
> *He is exalted, the King is exalted on high.*

("HE IS EXALTED")

DEVOTIONAL TEACHING

Twila's comments on "Running to the Rescue" touch on a second fundamental matter pertaining to biblical worship: fallen creatures cannot rescue themselves; only God can do that, and God has accomplished the rescue through Jesus Christ. For "God was reconciling the world to himself in Christ" (2 Cor. 5:19).

In the last chapter I pointed to the breakdown of relationship between God and human beings caused by Adam's choice to sin against God, a choice we all share.

In this chapter, I want to look at the restoration of relationship which prompts our response of praise and worship. As I have pointed out, the breakdown of our relationship with God is associated with one man, Adam, and the effect of his sin on the whole human race. On the other hand, the restoration of relationship focuses on one Man, Christ. The point is that Jesus Christ restored everything that was lost as a result of Adam's sin. He ran to the rescue and saved us.

In my attempts to understand worship, I have found the truth — that Jesus Christ must be the center of our worship — to be the single most important discovery of my studies. Jesus, by His death and resurrection, has reversed the human situation. He has conquered the powers of evil, defeated Satan, thrown down Hell, and opened the way to heaven. By doing the work of the Father, He is God's work of worship. Our work of worship is to respond to the Father in Jesus' name by the power of the Holy Spirit with thanksgiving. Let's look at this work of Jesus more thoroughly.

RECONCILED BY GOD AND MAN

In my seminary studies I learned that the human condition is so badly in need of repair that not one of us from the human family can run to the rescue. No one, that is, other than Christ. He chose to become one of us and to share completely in our humanity, except that He did not sin.

I don't think I began to appreciate the extent of the work of Christ in representing me and all of humanity until I took a course on Romans 5:12-21. In this course I was introduced to the biblical teaching of the First and Second Adam. I learned that as the First Adam did something to the human race, so the Second Adam did something for the human race. The First Adam brought sin, death and condemnation, but the Second Adam reversed this chain of events and brought righteousness, life, and justification. It was an inspiring truth to discover that as we all bear the image of the First Adam, so also we may choose to bear the image of the Second Adam. Paul put it this way: "And just as we have borne the likeness of the earthly man, so shall we bear the likeness of the man from heaven" (1 Cor. 15:49).

This theme of the victory of Christ over the powers of evil shows up in worship in the earliest known prayer of thanksgiving over the bread and wine, a prayer that was written down in the early third century by Hippolytus, a bishop in Rome. I love this ancient prayer over bread and wine because it speaks so forcibly about the reason we worship and give thanks to God in Jesus' name. Here is part of the text of that striking prayer:

"Who [Christ] fulfilling thy will and preparing for thee a holy people stretched forth his hands for suffering that He might release from suffering them who have believed in thee; who when He was betrayed to voluntary suffering that He might abolish death and rend the bonds of the devil and tread down hell . . . taking bread, etc. (*The Apostolic Tradition*, IV, 7-8).

In these words, the early church acknowledged that the work of Jesus is the only reason why worship is possible. We can only worship in Jesus' name because Jesus has dealt a decisive blow to the powers of evil, overcoming them in His death and resurrection. Only Jesus can and has run to our rescue.

THE UNIVERSAL SIGNIFICANCE OF JESUS' WORK

As I began to think more deeply about how the work of Christ reverses the human situation, I began to grasp the universal significance of the work of Christ, and this insight added depth to my worship.

It is this image of the Second Adam that brings out the universal significance of Jesus. The sin of the first man bore universal results by starting a chain of events that destroyed humanity's relationship with the entire created order. But the righteous obedience of the Second Adam, Christ, reversed that order of events and brought potential healing to all those broken relationships.

Paul referred to the universal effect of Jesus in his letter to the Colossian Christians: "For God was pleased to have all his fullness dwell in him, and through him to reconcile to himself all things, whether things on earth or things in heaven, by making peace through his blood, shed on the cross" (Col. 1:19-20). The reality is that the Creator Himself has entered into the creation that He might rescue it and bring healing to the broken relationships that characterize its fallenness. No wonder Paul could write these words of exaltation: "For from him and through him and to him are all things. To him be the glory forever! Amen" (Rom. 11:36). To acknowledge Jesus is to worship.

The early church expressed the wonder of this theme in its early hymns. Here are two examples:

> *Man fell from the divine and better life;*
> *though made in the image of God,*
> *through transgression he became wholly subject*
> *to corruption and decay.*
> *But now the wise creator fashions him anew;*
> *for he has been glorified.*
>
> (Dec. 25, Matains of the Eastern Church)

> *David foreseeing in the spirit*
> *the sojourn with men of the only begotten Son in the flesh,*
> *called the creation to rejoice with him,*
> *and prophetically lifted up his voice to cry:*
> *"Tabor and Herman shall rejoice in my name"*
> *For having gone up, O Christ,*
> *with thy disciples into Mount Tabor,*
> *thou wast transfigured,*
> *and hast made the nature that*
> *had grown dark in Adam*
> *to shine again as lightening.*
>
> (August 6, Transfiguration Vespers
> of the Eastern Church)

THE HISTORICAL SIGNIFICANCE OF JESUS' WORK

Not only does Christ's work parallel Adam's in its universal significance, but also in its historical significance. As Adam's sin initiated a chain of events that affected history, so Christ's death and resurrection set in motion another chain of events that take shape in history. And for this we give God thanks and exalt the name of Jesus in our worship.

We are born into and live our lives within an era of history. We are affected by the events of history. The image of God in us is expressed in history, in marriage, family, and work. Because we are historical, social creatures, and because we have perverted our social relationships, it follows that our redemption must take place in history in the context of our God-ordained tasks and human relationships. It is here, in life itself, that our broken relationships are expressed. It must be here, in life itself, that our restored relationship is accomplished. God's rescue operation in Jesus Christ happened in time, space, and history. God was here in Jesus Christ in real flesh and blood. He was crucified, died, was buried, and rose again. These acts, which occurred in history set into motion a new society, the church. And the church, the people who have been rescued, constitute a new history in the world.

Much of what we do in the worship of the church is a thankful recitation of the redemptive history of God running to the rescue. When I first discovered this fact, I began to look for this recitation everywhere and found it in Scripture, in songs, in prayers, in creeds, and in the thanksgiving given over bread and wine. For example, the Apostles Creed is really a historical recitation of salvation, a great cry of thanksgiving for God's great gift of salvation in Jesus Christ. Many of the great hymns of the church praise God for salvation by recounting God's great saving deeds. The prayers over bread and wine have always been accompanied by words of thanksgiving for God's saving deeds in Jesus Christ.

CHALLENGE

The challenge of this chapter is to gain a greater clarity about the centrality of Jesus in our worship.

To be biblical, our worship must always be in Jesus' name. Only Jesus is the true worship of the Father because only Jesus has healed the broken relationships of the world by running to its rescue.

Here is where the heart of the challenge lies: many people incorrectly think that worship is exclusively the praises they offer to the Father and that they are to work up a particular kind of emotion or feeling that will be pleasing to God. This mistaken notion of worship has resulted in numerous worship shipwrecks because people don't feel as deeply as they would like to feel and they think they haven't worshiped.

The truth is that we cannot offer anything that will please God because Jesus Christ has accomplished God's pleasure and re-established a relationship with God, a thing we cannot do.

How then should we worship? We worship when we respond to God in Jesus' name, when we respond to what God has done for us through Christ. We praise, exalt, glorify, and magnify God in and through Jesus by the power of the Holy Spirit. Our worship is in the remembering and in the giving of thanks.

When we remember God's saving deeds and give thanks, the feelings often become involved. Some people may weep; others may dance with joy. Being in a good relationship with God, a relationship established only by Jesus, is often felt deep within the inner recesses of the mind, the heart, and the soul, prompting the deepest feelings of the heart.

The challenge of this chapter is to grasp this principle of Christ-centered worship. It is not an easy principle to grasp because the human mind wants to take credit for the worship of God, just as the human mind wants to take credit for salvation. But the radical biblical doctrine of grace declares that Christ alone is our salvation

(Eph. 2:13) and Christ alone is our worship (Heb. 8-10). Our work in worship is to remember God's deeds of salvation and to give thanks. And this "remembering with thanksgiving" is the work of the body of Christ, the church, the theme of the next chapter.

CHAPTER FOUR

Worship Is the Work of the Church
"Worship is the ultimate expression of the church."

In this sanctuary
We have all beheld
Only You are holy
There is no one else
No one who is worthy
Worthy to sit upon the throne
In this sanctuary
We worship You alone

("IN THIS SANCTUARY")

INTERPRETATION

We included the word "sanctuary" in the title of this book because it carries so many different meanings. The word sanctuary brings thoughts of a safe place, a hiding place. For all of us, that safe place is in the Lord. We must turn to Him for refuge because the Lord is a strong and mighty tower.

The sanctuary is also the place where we worship. The smallest sanctuary is our own heart, that private place where we meet God all alone, hear the voice of God and respond. The sanctuary is also the gathering of believers for worship, whether it is a small gathering of five or six in a home, or a larger gathering in the local church. And, of course, I also like to think of my concerts as a gathering, a sanctuary, because the worship of the living God is always a central theme in my concerts.

I love to worship alone in the privacy of the space I have set aside for worship. But I also love to worship with others. I think one of the truly significant spiritual insights of the contemporary worship renewal is the recovery of the sense of corporate, or group worship.

I worship God through songs, but I'm learning that worship is much more than singing alone, my individual voice raised in worship. It's the response of the whole people to God, the response of the entire company of the redeemed.

What happens when people gather for corporate worship reminds me of going to my grandmother's house for Christmas. My grandmother's house had this special, wonderful, inviting smell to it. I get nostalgic when I think of that smell and of the whole atmosphere of being with my family at my grandparents.

For me, corporate worship is like going to Grandma's house. There is something really special about going to God's house with the family of God and meeting together to worship. Like my nostalgia for Grandmother's house, I sense that the church is rediscovering corporate worship in the house of God and that there is a new longing to gather together for worship in God's house.

What we do in God's house is expressed in "Let Them Praise." In God's house the response to God is from young and old, the high and the lowly, and the mighty and the poor. When we gather together, the thoughts of our hearts and the words of our mouth proclaim that God's name, God's throne, and God's love is above all names, all thrones, and all loves:

> *Lord, Your name is above any other name*
> *And forever will remain*
> *So let the words of my mouth*
> *And the thoughts in my heart*
> *Let them praise Your name*

Lord, Your throne is above any other throne
And forever will remain
So let the young and the old
Let the high and the low
Let them praise, let them praise
Let them praise Your name

Lord, Your love is above any other love
And forever will remain
So let us go with Your Word
To the ends of the earth
And let them praise, let them praise
Let them praise Your name

("LET THEM PRAISE")

DEVOTIONAL TEACHING

Twila is right that the sanctuary has many meanings, one of which is the people of God who have gathered to worship.

Unfortunately, the biblical notion of the church is sadly neglected by many Christians. This neglect doesn't arise out of anything personal; it's more a cultural matter.

The cultural issue is the permeation of individualism within the Western culture, and particularly the American culture. For example, the humanism of the Enlightenment proclaimed the autonomy of the individual when it insisted that "man is the measure of all things." Unfortunately this secular humanistic notion has permeated the American culture.

Gradually we Americans have cut ourselves off from the teaching of our dependence upon God and of the providence of God. We now think of ourselves as alone on an island with no one else around, having as our only alternative seizing the day and creating our own future. This dramatic commitment to individualism has affected American Christianity to the extent that we have privatized the Christian faith, making it a matter of the heart, the closet of our relationship to God. Consequently, worship for many people is understood exclusively in terms of individual worship. The concept of the community of public worship has become lost, and even when people come together collectively, the value of worship often continues to be expressed in forms of individual experience within the collective group.

In this chapter I want to share with you the third important lesson I've learned about worship. The first is that I cannot worship God because of my sinful condition. The second is that Christ is the worship of God and my worship or work is to remember the work of Christ and give thanks to God in His name. The third is that I am a member of a worldwide, two-thousand-year-old community of people on earth who continually offer corporate praise and worship to God. And in worship this people join the heavenly throng around the throne who continually sing "Holy, holy, holy is the Lord God Almighty, who was, and is, and is to come" (Rev. 4:8).

THE PROBLEM OF INDIVIDUALISM

As an American, I have always been affected by the concept of rugged individualism, not only in my personal life but also in my life as a Christian and a worshiper. Like others, I want to do it alone, and I want to do it my way. Unfortunately, this attitude is antithetical to Christianity, which is a community of people, and to public worship, which is the corporate action of God's people. I struggle with this conflict in me, and perhaps you do as well.

I found healing for my individualism when I began to understand the church as the continuation of the presence of Christ in the world. This is what it means, in part at least, to say that the church is the Body of Christ. But for me and for my worship a compelling feature of this teaching is the experience that this body is a new community, a new people where our broken relationships with God, self, neighbor, and nature are in the process of being healed through the work of Christ, which the church continually remembers in its worship. Let me explain this in greater detail by describing the context of our restored relationships, the church.

CORPORATE WORSHIP

We have seen that the work of Christ holds the key to the restoration of broken relationships. The consequences of Christ's victory over death are twofold. First, Christ broke the power of evil that holds sway over the lives of people and perpetuates the breakdown of relationships in every area of life. Second, people no longer live in bondage to sin, but are now free to choose to live in genuine community with God and fellow believers in the life of the church.

The work of Christ represented a new beginning. Paul wrote to the Corinthians that "the old has gone, the new has come" (2 Cor. 5:17). In the work of Christ, the world's opportunity to acknowledge God's sovereignty was being re-established, and the possibility of a new and genuine life for humanity was being made available. Jesus had come that "they may have life, and have it to the full" (John 10:10).

The context in which these restored relationships are to take place is no nebulous and ethereal sphere, but the church. The church is the people of God on earth. It is the visible, tangible, historical, and social body of people who belong to Christ. These are the people who are related to God and to the world in a new way. Therefore, it is in the context of the household of God, the church, where restored relationships must begin. This perspective contains numerous implications for worship. But before we can look more closely at the implications, we need to get a clearer picture of the church as the focus of restored relationships. In the church and in its worship, the broken relationships between us and God, our inner self, our neighbor, and nature experience a God-given healing.

All broken relationships have been restored. And if that is not enough, God has placed us in a community of people where we are given the opportunity to work out these broken relationships. And this community, an "earthed" community is a foretaste of the heavenly community, our abiding and eternal city.

IN THE CHURCH AND IN ITS WORSHIP ALL BROKEN RELATIONSHIPS BEGIN TO FIND HEALING

I want to comment on how our broken relationships with God, our inner self, our neighbor, and with nature find healing in the worship of the church because I have found that the understanding of this truth has given both breadth and depth to my worship.

THE HEALING OF OUR RELATIONSHIP WITH GOD

The first truth I discovered is that the healing of my broken relationship with God is symbolized in baptism, an act which from the very beginning of the church has been part of worship. I remember, for example, how the repair of my broken relationship was symbolized in my own baptism. Before I was baptized but standing there in the water, my father, the minister said to me, "Robert, do you renounce the works of the devil?" I said, "I do," and I was baptized in the name of the Father, Son, and Holy Spirit. In the early church when this question was asked, the person to be baptized spit in the direction of Satan (west) as a sign of breaking a relationship with Satan and all the forces of evil.

Baptism is the passage rite into the body of Christ, the church. Anyone who has been justified by faith and has, as Paul stated in Romans 5:1, "peace with God through our Lord Jesus Christ" is now called to an identification with Christ through a baptism "into his death" (Rom. 6:3). Baptism, especially by immersion, is a powerful material symbol of what actually happens when a relationship with God is restored. It is the material symbol of our spiritual union with Christ. As Paul says, "If we have been united with him like this in his death, we will certainly also be united with him in his resurrection" (Rom. 6:5).

When Jesus commanded His disciples to, "'Therefore go and make disciples of all nations, baptizing them in the name of the Father and of the Son and of the Holy Spirit'" (Matt. 28:19), He had in mind that indissoluble union between Himself and the church that is expressed in a restored relationship. This is borne out by His concluding statement: "'And surely I am with you always, to the very end of the age'" (Matt. 28:20). God's presence is both personal and corporate in the church. The life of the believer is lived out in the context of the church, Christ's body. Thus, the statement of the church father, Cyprian (A.D. 250), that "he who has not the church for his mother has not God for his father" stands. Baptism symbolizes our entrance into the church, the community of God's restored people.

THE HEALING OF THE INNER SELF

Next, I discovered that the broken relationship which I experienced in my inner self and the loss of self-worth which came from that ruptured inner self found a place of healing in the church and in its worship.

Self-worth is derived not from anything we have done but from the realization that we are remade in the image of God. Paul spoke of the Christian as "to be made new in the attitude of your minds; and to put on the new self, created to be like God in true righteousness and holiness" (Eph. 4:23-24). Having been remade in the image of God, we receive a restored sense of our task and function in the world. We no longer see ourselves as a mere cog in the machine or a cork tossed about on the ocean, but instead we may regard ourselves in relation to God's calling. Our self-acceptance is rooted in the recognition of the part we are to play in the drama of the world.

But this self-realization does not take place in a vacuum. Rather, it comes to fruition in the church and in its worship. Paul wrote of the varieties of "gifts," the "different kinds of service . . . [and] working" that are given for "the common good" (1 Cor. 12:4-7). What Paul was expressing here, and throughout 1 Corinthians 12 – 14, is the principle that each of us from the body of Christ brings gifts that are profitable to all. No one is without value or not important to the body. Everyone has something to contribute. This means, of course, that in the church, we need to help each person find his or her unique gift and exercise it to the benefit of all. When the gifts God has given to us are accepted and used in the church, our own sense of self-worth is intensified.

HEALING WITH OUR NEIGHBOR

A third result of Jesus' death and resurrection is the experience of community that we find in the church. We are a community of people, brothers and sisters, whom Paul calls the "household of faith" (Gal. 6:10, NKJV). We are part of a family that crosses generational lines, cultural barriers, and rises above sexual distinctions. I know, of course, that I'm speaking here of the goal of this community which will be achieved in the new heavens and the new earth. And I'm saddened by the many divisions in the body of Christ, just as you are saddened. But let me give you an example of this "family" at its best.

Recently, I was at a conference in Oklahoma City sponsored by the Society of St. Barnabas the Encourager, a society committed to unity in the church. At that conference there were clergy and people from the Orthodox, Catholic, and Protestant churches including main line Protestants, Evangelicals, Pentecostals, and Charismatics.

The most moving part of this conference for us all was when we worshiped together. We recited the common history of our salvation and offered thanks to God through Jesus Christ. Here our theological divisions and barriers of language, culture, and sex were replaced with our unified praises of God. And in this worship we prefigured and even experienced a touch of heavenly worship.

Healing with Nature

Finally, our broken relationship with nature finds a healing expression in the church and in its worship. Paul wrote of the renewal of creation in Romans:

> ". . . the creation itself will be liberated from its bondage to decay and brought into the glorious freedom of the children of God. We know that the whole creation has been groaning as in the pains of childbirth right up to the present time. Not only so, but we ourselves, who have the first fruits of the Spirit, groan inwardly as we wait eagerly for our adoption as sons, the redemption of our bodies. For in this hope we were saved. . . ." (Rom. 8:21-24)

The ancient church had a far more in-depth understanding of the restored relationships of humanity with nature than the modern church has. First, their consciousness was informed by a strong sense of the demonic presence in nature. Paul's insight that "our struggle is not against flesh and blood, but against the rulers, against the authorities, against the powers of this dark world and against the spiritual forces of evil in the heavenly realms" (Eph. 6:12) was taken far more seriously in the early church than it is taken in the modern scientific world.

The liturgies of ancient Christianity symbolically expressed Christ's victory over the power that evil exercises in nature. The Blessing of Epiphany, for example, proclaims God's power and control over the universe and affirms that humanity is no longer a slave to evil forces. Here is a prayer from the early church that expresses the restored relationship of nature:

> *The immaterial powers tremble before thee;*
> *the sun praises thee;*
> *and the moon worships thee;*
> *the stars are thy servants;*
> *and light bows to thy will;*
> *the tempests tremble and the springs adore thee.*
> *Thou dost spread out the heavens like a tent;*
> *thou didst set the land upon the waters . . .*
> *(therefore) heading the depth of thy compassion,*
> *O Master,*
> *thou couldst not bear to see humanity defeated by the devil,*
> *and so thou didst come and didst save us . . .*
> *thou didst free the children of our nature. . . .*

(SEE JOHN MYENDORFF, *BYZANTINE THEOLOGY*, P. 135)

When the early church blessed water and sprinkled it on the land, plants, or houses, they were not following some pagan mystical rite. They were acting on a theological insight that nature had been redeemed. This action of the sanctification of nature is a proclamation of the renewal of creation through Jesus Christ and, therefore, of the believer's relationship to creation.

This concept of the sanctification of nature is also poignantly seen in the blessing of bread and wine. When bread and wine have been set aside by the word of prayer to represent Christ's body and blood, no more dramatic presentation of the redemption of the natural elements can be made.

CHALLENGE

We are now digging more deeply into the subject of public worship, and we see that it is far more profound than singing songs and offering individual praise to God.

The challenge we wish to present here is that worship is the true expression of the church, God's people on earth. Worship is not only something that the church does, but worship is what the church is. Worship reveals the very nature of the church, for the church at worship is a prefigured experience of the ultimate goal of human history. The church at worship is the presence of the future.

The Scriptures teach that at the end of the world God will bring into being the new heavens and the new earth. The Scriptures also teach that the church at worship now is an earthly expression of this ultimate goal of the church, which will be realized in the new heavens and the new earth. So in worship, heaven makes an appearance, it comes down among us, and draws us into the experience of a restored relationship with God, with self, with neighbor, and with nature.

It is this vision which we enact in the church when we worship, and this vision shapes and forms us into the society of strangers, aliens, and sojourners in this world. This world is not our final resting place. And worship gives us a taste of the heaven to come.

Allow me to close this chapter with an example of the future orientation of worship. It comes from African American worship. As you know, deep in black genetic history is a sense of dislocation with the culture of this world. On the plantation blacks were "niggers," a term that meant they were nobody. They could be sold on the block like cattle, children could be sent off never to be seen again, and the plantation owner could do whatever he pleased with their lives.

But when the blacks assembled to do church they entered a new world, the promised land. Here they were relocated with God and no one was "nigger." Everyone was "brother" and "sister," and the reality of a new world, a new order of things was experienced, even though it was ever so brief.

So, here is our challenge. Like our African American brothers and sisters, let's learn how to do church in our worship. Let's enter into that heavenly realm and worship with the angels, the archangels, and all the heavenly host. For in worship we are momentarily united with heavenly worship and gather with the saints around the throne and do church. And in this momentary experience of the heaven which is to come, the church now is a prefiguring of the healing brought to all broken relationships—with God, self, neighbor, and nature—and an actual experience of this healing now in our earthly life.

CHAPTER FIVE

In Worship We Remember and Give Thanks
"God reaches out to us and for us.
Our challenge is to worship intentionally."

We will glorify the King of kings
We will glorify the Lamb
We will glorify the Lord of lords
Who is the great I Am

Lord Jehovah reigns in majesty
We will bow before the throne
We will worship Him in righteousness
We will worship Him alone

He is Lord of heaven, Lord of earth
He is Lord of all who live
He is Lord above the universe

All praise to Him we give
O Hallelujah to the King of kings
Hallelujah to the Lamb
Hallelujah to the Lord of lords
Who is the Great I Am

("WE WILL GLORIFY")

INTERPRETATION

I understand our worship to be a response to God. Worship is not only a response to the character of God, but also to what God has done to restore our lives, to touch us, to heal us, and to make us whole.

All of my worship songs are a response to God's saving and healing presence. "We Will Glorify," "Lamb of God," "He Is Exalted," "We Bow Down," and "For the Glory of the Lord" all belong in the category of worship songs because they are primarily response songs. I think that's why these songs are so popular—they provide a vehicle for people to offer their response of praise and thanksgiving to God. And, while I don't want to be mystical about it, I really feel these songs are special gifts from God.

For example, I wasn't writing music in the genre of "We Will Glorify," but all of a sudden the words and music were there. I don't mean that I closed my eyes and the pen moved. But, really, it was only one notch more difficult than that. The Lord allowed me to be involved in the process, but it was very obvious to me that I wasn't the one who wrote it.

Sometimes people refer to "We Will Glorify" and my other worship songs as "anointed." I know that word gets used a lot, but what I think Christians mean by it is that they recognize God's Spirit in the song.

Both the words and the music of "We Will Glorify" put me in mind of the majesty of God. Experiencing the grandeur of God is different from the emotional response of an intimate worship song. A sense of awe rises up in my heart because my praise of the King of kings and Lord of lords not only associates me with the great I Am but is even acceptable and pleasing to the one who sits on the throne. So, every time I sing this hymn-like song, I'm personally moved.

I'm so grateful to know that "We Will Glorify" has the same effect on groups of people who sing the song together. I'm frequently thanked by people who tell me that this song and my other worship songs are actually gifts to them because these songs give them words of praise. It also makes them feel, they say, like they are members of a much larger community who are all praising God. I think it's because worship songs connect people with the heavenly throng, the whole community of angels, archangels, cherubim, and seraphim who continually offer their praises to God.

Often when I sing these worship songs in concert, the audience becomes very quiet. The first time this happened, I thought to myself, "They didn't like the concert tonight." But after the concert people came to me and said, "The words of your songs really spoke to me tonight," or "We were all really touched by your songs; some of us even wept." I began to realize that much of what is happening in my concerts is not just an emotional reaction. People are being moved to offer their thanks to God for Christ and what He did. That's worship. These incidents make me realize that worship happens in the heart as the people respond to the God who is present through song, sermon, communion, prayer, and the many other ways God comes to us in worship. As we lift up our hearts, voices, and our hands, our whole person responds to the God who is speaking and acting in our midst.

You are Lord of creation and Lord of my life
Lord of the land and the sea
You are Lord of the heavens before there was time
And Lord of all lords You will be

We bow down and we worship You, Lord
We bow down and we worship You, Lord
We bow down and we worship You, Lord
Lord of all lords You will be

You are King of creation and King of my life
King of the land and the sea
You are King of the heavens before there was time
And King of all kings You will be

We bow down and we crown You the King
We bow down and we crown You the King
We bow down and we crown You the King
King of all kings You will be.

("We Bow Down")

DEVOTIONAL TEACHING

Twila's song "We Will Glorify" is one of those songs that has taken up residence in me and dwells in my subconscious. I find myself frequently singing the song silently or humming it in my heart as a response of praise and worship to God. Worship is just that; it is a continual response of praise on our lips and in our lives.

The key word for us to meditate on is response. Worship, whether it is private worship or public worship, is always a response to the God who is and to the God who acts.

For this reason it is important for us to recognize that we never initiate worship. It is God who initiates worship, because it is always God who reaches out to us. Our role in worship is to respond.

In the next few pages I want to comment on the ways God reaches out to us, so that we can understand better how we can articulate our response to God.

God Reaches Out to Us Where We Are

The central concern of Scripture, the book of worship, is to relate how people may be saved from the power of sin and enter into fullness of life. In this sense, Christianity is not unique. All religions of the world are concerned with salvation of one kind or another. In the ancient world, for example, there were numerous redemption myths, each of which offered a plan of salvation.

Because of this, I find myself asking, "What makes the Christian religion unique?" One unique feature of Christianity is that it is a historical redemption; in contrast, the myths and New Age religions of the world offer a way of escape from this world. Biblical religion is a religion of this world as well as of the next. For example, the Israelites were redeemed from Egypt so they could worship as God's people on earth. The hope of Christianity, therefore, differs from the myths and New Age religion in that it is a religion for this world as well as the next.

The teaching that God reaches for us whatever our circumstances in life lies at the very heart of the Scripture story and, therefore, of our worship. The whole history of the Scriptures attests to this principle. God initiated a relationship with Abraham, then with the patriarchs, with Israel through the covenant at Mt. Sinai, with the prophets, and then in Jesus Christ. Now God continues to search us out through the work of the Holy Spirit. The same God who has been at work throughout history initiating a relationship with fallen creatures is present in our worship. He is continuing to establish, maintain, repair, and transform our relationship with Him.

I was explaining the principle that God reaches out to us in the circumstances of our life to a group of students at Northern Baptist Seminar in the Chicago area where I was teaching a course on worship. I especially urged them to see how God's saving work, which is recited in worship, needs to be connected with the circumstances of the people in a local congregation.

I suggested they make this connection in prayer, although songs and preaching do the same (note soul music and black preaching, in particular). As they worked on this project, they were soon making connections with all kinds of problems in their churches: broken homes, sickness, unwanted pregnancies, abuse, domestic violence, and many other issues. In this way they were getting in touch with the brokenness of life and seeing how God reaches out in the circumstances of our lives. They began to understand how God's past action could be proclaimed as God's present action and how healing could begin to take root in the lives of their people as they experienced the power of God's healing presence in worship.

The point is that the God who reached out to Abraham, to Moses, to Israel, and to the Gentiles in their circumstances of life, reaches out to us where we are. Authentic worship is God reaching out to us where we are, and, like the characters of the Bible, we reach back to God in response. There is no essential difference. When we come to God in worship, we come as Zaccheus, as the woman taken in adultery, as the ruler who seeks God at night, as blind Bartimaeus, as the woman who touched the hem of Jesus' garment, as the demoniac, and as the frightened disciples on the tossing sea. God reaches for us where we are, and we respond.

GOD REACHES OUT TO US THROUGH LANGUAGE

One of the wonders of the Christian faith and of worship is that God reaches out to us in ways that we can understand and grasp. God is a communicator who comes to us and meets us in our own language.

The Scriptures abound with references about God's direct and indirect use of language as a means of communication. God spoke to Adam in the Garden of Eden (Gen. 2:16) as well as after the Fall (Gen. 3:18). He spoke to Cain (Gen. 4:6-15) and later to Noah (Gen. 9:1). In the history of Israel God's direct communication through language became less frequent. God began to speak through prophets (Exod. 19:9) who spoke the word of the Lord to the people. Throughout the Old Testament and particularly in the prophetic books, refrains such as "thus saith the Lord" or "the word of the Lord came to me saying" appear repeatedly. A study of these people shows that they did, in fact, hear. They may not have obeyed, but that the word of the Lord was communicated, there can be no doubt.

Because God reaches out to us in language and in everyday speech, the speech of worship, God finds the language of our response an acceptable offering of praise and worship.

As we think about the significance of language in worship, we may consider one of the major gifts of worship renewal today to be found in the language of response expressed in many of the new worship songs. I realize many worship songs are superficial and have no power to facilitate the praises of God's people. But I also think there are a number of songs that introduce a new language of response. For example, "We Will Glorify" and "He Is Exalted" use language and music in such a provocative way that people are able to release their responses of praise using the very medium that God used to reach us, language.

Also, throughout the history of the church, worshipers have responded to God's proclamation in brief statements of praise such as Amen!, Alleluia!, Thanks be to God!, Hosanna!, Maranatha!, and Abba, Father! The current worship renewal is restoring this language of praise, and I believe our experience of responding to God's grace in worship is being deepened and enhanced by a return to these biblical acclamations.

God Reaches Out to Us Through Imagination

An important feature of the Christian faith and of worship is that it never denies who we are. Because we are God's people made in God's image, God reaches out toward us in the fullness of who we are. For example, God is a God of imagination. Everything that is, God made out of nothing. God formed the world and gave it shape and color. Every blade of grass, every cloud formation, every insect, all the colors of the rainbow, and the intricacies of the human body and mind were all imagined and created by God. Because God is a God of imagination who made imaginative people, God reaches out to us through the imagination, and we respond to God in worship through the use of our God-given imagination.

There are numerous accounts in Scripture of God's reaching out to us through the imagination. This visionary material of Scripture has gained wide usage in the church and has resulted in the development of liturgy, music, and art as responses of praise and worship. Think, for example, of the images present in the vision of Isaiah, who saw the Lord:

> . . . seated on a throne, high and exalted, and the train of his robe filled the temple. Above him were seraphs, each with six wings: With two wings they covered their faces, with two they covered their feet, and with two they were flying. And they were calling to one another: "Holy, holy, holy is the Lord Almighty; the whole earth is full of his glory." (Isa. 6:1-3)

This vision, along with a similar one of John's in Revelation 4 and 5, has continued to inspire Christians throughout the centuries. The vision of heavenly worship became a basis for the development of worship within the early church. The beauty and pageantry of Byzantine worship, for example, is patterned after the glory and majesty surrounding Christ on His throne. The refrain "Holy, holy, holy" which is central to Roman Catholic, Eastern Orthodox, and Anglican worship, has inspired a major hymn in Protestant worship and a number of new choruses. The centrality of the throne has inspired works of art and architecture.

Other imaginative visions that have had a similar effect on the church include Ezekiel's (see chapters 1—3, 8—11), Jeremiah's (see chapter 13), Daniel's (see 1:17, 2:19, and chapters 7—10), Amos' (see chapters 7—9), and John's (see the book of Revelation). In these visions, pictures, portraits, and demonstrations, God reaches us through our imaginations.

But what does all of this have to do with our worship? How do we respond to God in our imagination? I think it is important for us to recognize how our imagination is used in worship. Processions, baptisms, the celebration of the Table of the Lord, the great festivals of Christmas and Easter all touch our imagination. That is, they are visual, tactile, colorful, action-oriented acts of worship that usually recall God's saving events and literally bring us to the throne of God to worship not only with our hearts, our bodies, and our minds, but also with our imaginations. In this way we return God's gift of imagination to God in an act of response, and that response is our worship.

God Reaches to Us by Becoming One of Us

Even though God reaches out to us in the circumstances of life through language and imagination, the climax of God's seeking us out is in the Incarnation. Here, in this great act of humility, God became one of us and communicated with us face to face.

Given the importance of the Incarnation as a means through which God communicates with us, we must ask, then, about the implications of the Incarnation for worship.

I first began to grasp the meaning of form in worship when I understood the truth of the Incarnation. The truth is that God did not meet us in some ethereal, nontangible way; instead, He came to us in the material form of a human person. This tangible presence of God in the form of flesh, which is what the Incarnation is, establishes forever the significance of form for any continued contact with God.

Let me illustrate what I'm trying to say by drawing on an example from the early church. In the first and second century a heretical Christian sect known as the Gnostics insisted that the Incarnation was an apparition. They claimed that God did not become flesh, but that Jesus was a phantom appearance. The reason they argued against God's taking human form is because they thought the material, tangible creation was intrinsically evil, therefore, God, the immaterial one, could not participate in materiality without being contaminated. Orthodox Christianity argued otherwise. Drawing from the biblical tradition, they insisted that the God who became incarnate was the same God who created the world. For them there was no contradiction in the notion that the non-material could participate in the material, the Divine could participate in the human.

The implication of biblical Christianity is that God, who met us in the Incarnation, continues to meet us in the visible, tangible forms of life. Consequently, the incarnational principle affirms that God meets us in our worship in the very setting of the assembled people, in the language of Scripture, preaching and prayer, in the mystery of sound and sight, and in the tangible signs of bread and wine.

When I understood this incarnational principle, I was easily able to appreciate and to experience the teaching of God's manifest presence in worship. I now believe that the God who is "with us" in the Incarnation is now really and truly present with us in our worship. God, as the psalmist says, "inhabits the praises of his people." He becomes present to us through all the forms of our worship in keeping with the promise that "where two or three come together in my name, there am I with them" (Matt. 18:20). God is present in worship to make available to us the benefit of God's saving work. God is there in a manifest presence to touch our lives, to save us, to heal us, and to make us whole.

CHALLENGE

The challenge of this chapter is to recognize that our worship is always a response to the God who reaches out to us. We do not worship in a vacuum. We respond to the God who speaks and acts.

What we respond to in worship is the God of our salvation. God, who has been initiating a relationship with fallen creatures, continues to initiate a relationship with us today in worship. Just as

God has always met people where they are, spoken to them in the language of everyday speech, reached them in their imaginations, and become present to them face to face, so God continues today to reach us where we are, in language, through imagination, and in His manifest presence.

Our challenge is to worship intentionally. We should say to ourselves, "I'm going to respond to God out of my circumstances; I'll hide nothing from Him. As God speaks to me, I'll respond with the language of praise; as God becomes present to me in the imagination of worship, I'll let my own imagination be free to be at the throne of God; and as God meets me face to face in the manifest presence, I'll bow down and glorify His matchless name." As we do these things with sincerity and integrity, and respond to God authentically, we are doing worship.

PART II

The Practice of Worship

INTRODUCTION

Part II of In This Sanctuary *is organized around what
we actually do in worship.
In the New Testament church worship was ordered around two focuses,
described in Acts 2:42: the apostolic teaching
and the breaking of bread. These acts of worship were expressed in
the context of prayer and fellowship.
Gradually, as the church developed its worship, the church added acts
of entrance and acts of dismissal.
This resulted in what we call the fourfold pattern of worship:*

—

The people of God assemble.

—

The people of God hear the Word of the Lord.

—

*The people of God remember
and give thanks at the table of the Lord.*

—

The people of God are sent forth into the world.

—

*We will explore these four acts in the following chapters, and in keeping
with the thrust of this book, we will approach
these four acts from a reflective and devotional viewpoint rather than
a "how to" point of view. We hope to provide insights and
understandings that will not only enrich
your experience of worship but also empower your Christian life
as you continue to discover* lex orandi; lex credendi est *—the rule of prayer
is the rule of faith. As you worship, so you believe.*

CHAPTER SIX

Gathering in the Sanctuary
"We are assembled because God has called us into being and
intends to shape us into the 'light of the world.'"

> *We shall assemble on the mountain*
> *We shall assemble at the throne*
> *With humble hearts into His presence*
> *We bring an offering of song*
> *Glory and honor and dominion*
> *Unto the Lamb, unto the King*
> *Oh hallelujah, hallelujah*
> *We sing the song of the Redeemed*

("WE SHALL ASSEMBLE")

INTERPRETATION

There is a passage of Scripture in Isaiah that I love. Isaiah
speaks of the people streaming to the mountain of the Lord to
worship. He says, "The mountain of the Lord's temple will be
established as chief among the mountains; it will be raised above the
hills, and all nations will stream to it" (Isa. 2:2).

Streaming to the mountain to worship is a prominent
theme throughout the body of Christ. Isaiah 2:2 is also a
foundational Scripture of Youth with a Mission (Arkansas), which is
my home fellowship.

When I wrote "We Shall Assemble," I had Isaiah's marvelous
picture in mind. I saw all the people of God streaming toward the
mountain where they would come into the presence of God.

I love the word pictures of the Scripture, and I have always been
fascinated by the visual image of Israel coming to the mountain with

Moses to meet God. I think it is fascinating how this concept of assembling at the mountain has always been associated with worship in the Scriptures. There is the image of worship at the Mount of Olives, at Mt. Tabor when Christ was transfigured, and, of course, Revelation 4 and 5 pictures our ultimate worship before the throne of God. I like to picture God's throne as having mountain-like characteristics.

The biblical notion of assembling could apply to any fellowship. In all the churches of the world the people are streaming in and then streaming out. We stream to the fellowship of our church to worship; there in that place, at that mountain of God, we are built up, established, equipped, encouraged, challenged. Then we are sent out to go and spread the Kingdom of God.

I see the content of "We Shall Assemble" as speaking to what we do when we stand at the foot of God's mountain. Picture this: we have streamed in from all parts of our city or town to assemble, and there in the gathering we bring an offering of praise and worship. Our song joins the great eternal song of the heavenlies as we gather around the throne with that great company of saints. We lift our voices together with them—crying, shouting, and singing, "To him who sits on the throne and to the Lamb be praise and honor and glory and power, for ever and ever!" (Rev. 5:13).

When I sing "We Shall Assemble," I am always moved by the pictures of King and dominion. Christ is our King, and someday He will exercise His rule, His dominion, over the entire world.

I know that when I'm among the assembled people that God is here in our midst. The King is here seeking to rule in our hearts right now. So this concept that where two or three are gathered, there He is in our midst is a powerful truth. It challenges us because sometimes when we gather for worship, we simply go through the motions. I know I've done that a number of times, and others have told me they have done the same. But I remind myself and others that whenever the people of God gather in a theater, in an arena, or in a church for worship, God is there.

That's why I often say in an opening prayer "Lord, we don't take lightly the fact that You're here." I don't want to come into the presence of the King of kings, the Lord of lords, the Creator and Redeemer of the universe in a nonchalant, casual, and impertinent way. No, I want to come before God in all humility recognizing I am a mere creature and He is holiness. He is the Creator.

To me this is what it means to assemble — coming into the presence of the King with humility and an attitude of praise. I tried to capture this posture of openness in my song "Hosanna." Come, the song says, honor God who is worthy of our praise; join all God's people and the entire creation as together we sing the almighty praises of God.

Hosanna, He is honored
Holy, holy, He is worthy
Hosanna, hallelujah
Holy, holy, King of kings

As the stars shine in the heavens
We declare the earth shall sing

Hosanna, He is honored
Holy, holy, He is worthy
Hosanna, hallelujah
Holy, holy, King of kings

("Hosanna")

DEVOTIONAL TEACHING

Recently I visited one of America's largest mega churches. I'm not a "mega church person" myself, preferring a smaller worshiping community, but occasionally I enjoy the particular kind of challenge the larger church provides.

One of those challenges is simply getting into the parking lot and then making the journey into the church. On this particular occasion I was struck by the enormous number of cars streaming from four corners of the area down a long driveway. There were literally hundreds of cars in sight, hurriedly moved on by dozens of policemen and car attendants dressed in yellow uniforms with red flag lights and walkie talkies. If I hadn't known better, I would have assumed that this was the parking lot for the World Series or an NBA championship game.

The person I was riding with, equally struck by this phenomenon that looked like the entire city streaming into worship, burst out, "Look at this, church has already begun!"

His point was well-made. Indeed worship had already begun in the act of assembling. Getting up, getting dressed, getting into your car, and getting to church for worship are the first stage of worship. You are already worshiping!

In the next few pages I want to reflect on the act of assembling, which is the first act of worship we do. I want to probe its biblical meaning, its theological significance, and its political symbolism. And I want you to see the spiritual significance of the act of simply coming together for worship.

The Biblical Meaning of Assembly

The word "assembly" simply means to come together. It can be used to describe any gathering of people for study, for social purposes, or for worship. But in the Scripture the word assumes a very specific spiritual connotation.

The word is used to refer to God's summoning the people together for worship. The key here is that it is God who summons the people to worship. Assembly itself is primarily an act of God, a divine action. And the people who come together do so as an act of response to God's bidding.

The first instance of the spiritual significance of assembly occurred at Mt. Sinai when God gathered Israel at the foot of the mountain for the first recorded public worship in Scripture (Exod. 24:1-8).

God had just brought the descendants of Abraham out of Egypt where they had been in bondage for years to the pharaohs, who had made them slaves and servants of their bidding. Now God was to enter into covenant with them. God was to become their God, and they were to become God's people in a solemn assembly marked by the reading of the Book of the Covenant and the ratification of the agreement between them through the shedding of blood.

This meeting and this covenant were in no way initiated by the Israelites. It was solely and completely God's doing.

The text of the meeting begins with these profound words, "Then he [God] said to Moses, 'Come up to the Lord . . . you are to worship'" (Exod. 24:1). Starting at this point and from henceforth, no assembly of Israel is convoked without the recognition that it is God who calls the people together.

This same theme is carried over into the New Testament. Paul uses the word "synaxis" (1 Cor. 11) to describe the gathering of people for worship. The literal translation of this word is to come together, and it means the same thing as the Old Testament word to assemble.

Today, like then, when we assemble to worship, it is because God has called us. We come only in response to God's calling, having within ourselves no power whatsoever to call into being and to actualize the body of Christ. This is God's doing and God's doing alone.

THEOLOGICAL SIGNIFICANCE OF ASSEMBLY

I don't think the assembly of people at worship is fully understood until we grasp that this community is a significant and unique group of people among all the peoples of the entire world. The assembled people are the people of God, a social construct, which, like no other social body in the world, represents what the world ought to be.

To understand this feature of the assembled people of God, we need to see the assembly against the backdrop of the biblical story of Creation, the Fall, redemption, and consummation.

When God created Adam and Eve, the original family, God's ideal was a society of people who would live in obedience to God's will, a society of people who would have dominion over the world, a people committed to till and keep the garden of Eden (Gen. 2:15). God gave the world to Adam and Eve and appointed them to be the keepers, the caretakers of the world.

But the Fall introduced a drastic change in God's original plan. Now humanity, rather than doing the will of God, turned against God, against God's will, against God's desire for creation and for society, culture, and civilization.

And, instead of unfolding culture under God, humanity became obedient to the powers of the evil one and created a culture that reflected their fallen condition.

Soon the world became full of evil: hate, greed, lust, murder, envy, strife among people, division among the nations, the creation of false gods, and the worship and service of all that is anti-God became the norm.

In this context, God acted to create a new people, a beginning again of civilization, a people who would live in obedience to God's will, a people who would worship and serve the living God.

Augustine, the great fourth century theologian of the church, captured the significance of this division of people in the title of his classic work *The City of God*. The presupposition of his entire book is that in the world there are two histories—the history of the city of man that issues forth from Cain the murderer, and the history of the city of God that finds its origin in Able who sought to do the will of God.

The story of the Scriptures is the story of God calling forth a new people—Abraham, the patriarchs, Israel, the prophets, and the church. These are the people who are called to stand in the midst of a society that follows the way of Cain.

When we Christians gather, we gather as the people of the Christ Event. We are the people of the new creation, the people of the beginning again of God's intention for the creation. And we gather to enact the story of God, to be reminded of God's intention for the world, of the fall of humanity, of God's gracious intervention in Jesus Christ to overcome evil, and of His establishment of a new people who will do His will on earth as in heaven.

This assembled people, then, is no mere collection of like-minded people, but the salt and light of the world gathered to enact the meaning of their existence and to be continually shaped by the politics of the kingdom.

THE POLITICAL SYMBOLISM OF ASSEMBLY

When the Christ Event is seen as the source of the new creation, the political depth of the assembly becomes a matter of utmost importance.

The political nature of the assembled people is very different from the political expression assumed by many contemporary churches. Unfortunately the church is frequently politicized by those who wish to align it to the political agendas of either the right or the left. God's agenda for the church is very different from that of either the Republican or the Democratic party or of any other worldly political agenda. This does not mean that a Christian cannot be a Republican or a Democrat. What it means is that God's ultimate goal in history is of a completely different nature than worldly politics. And the Christian, first and foremost, serves God's agenda, the agenda which it assembles to hear and to live by.

This political agenda of God is grounded in the historical event (Christ Event) through which the new people are called into being. God's political agenda is fulfilled in the future event, the new heavens and the new earth, where His social and political ideal of a world living under His rule (the Kingdom) will be realized.

In the Old Testament, Israel as a social and political community prefigured the church. Israel, called into being by God in the Exodus Event, was a new creation in the midst of a secular world and body politic, and they were called by God to be the new people moving toward the Promised Land. When they assembled, they came together to renew the covenant, to be instructed in their calling, and to be shaped as the future people in the present.

When the church assembles, it assembles as a people of the spiritual overthrow of the powers of evil. In the assembly the politics of God's Kingdom has found a manifestation in the world. The assembly gathers to hear of the overthrow of the kingdom of evil, to be formed by the new ethic of Jesus, to be empowered to live the new life of Christ in the world, and to proclaim by word and deed what the people of the new heavens and the new earth will be like.

CHALLENGE

The challenge of this chapter lies in our need to rediscover the biblical and deeply radical meaning of the assembly.

We need, first of all, to put away all our superficial notions of "counting heads" or "entertaining the crowds" and recover the fact that we are assembled because God has called us into being and intends to shape us into the "light of the world," the "salt of the earth."

Having swept away the wrong notions of assembling, we need to recover the purpose of the assembly: telling the story, rehearsing the meaning of human history, learning our place in the world, responding to God with thanksgiving in our hearts and in our lives, and allowing ourselves to become shaped into the people of God.

When we understand our coming together in this way, we will not only have understood what it means to assemble, but what it means to be the assembly at worship.

Remember this the next time you roll into the parking lot of the church. The powers of evil should be trembling at the sight. For here is a visual image of the people of the overcoming event gathering to hear once again about how the powers of evil are bound, dethroned, and doomed to ultimate destruction. And here, once again, these people have assembled to be formed and shaped by the politics of the new kingdom, the politics of love and service to one another.

CHAPTER SEVEN

Hearing the Word
"The word we hear and live by is the Word we worship."

I will wait on the Lord
I will wait for His word
Because I fear His holy name
I will wait
I will wait
I will wait on the Lord
I will wait for His word
Before I move, before I speak
Perfect wisdom I will seek
And I will wait as long as it takes
I will wait on the Lord
I will wait on the Lord

("I WILL WAIT")

INTERPRETATION

Not long ago, my sister, Angie, and I flew into Chicago where I was to do a television interview the next day. It was one of those long and tiring days, and it was quite late at night when we arrived.

The van that was to pick us up wasn't there, so I called to inform the driver of our arrival and to request a pickup. The driver was very casual and not at all assuring about the speed with which he would arrive. He didn't know where the keys were to the van, he said. So he couldn't give me an estimate of how long it would be before he could pick us up.

I was really discouraged, to say the least. So I said to my sister, "We'll wait fifteen minutes, and that's all. If he doesn't arrive by then, we will take a taxi."

I tell you this story because I think we do the same thing to God. We say, "OK God, You have this much time to come into our presence and speak. If You don't come in the time we have allotted, we'll take things into our own hands."

I think my song "I Will Wait" speaks to our gathering at the mountain. We have come here to respond to God with praise and worship, but we have also come to the mountain to wait. Worship is often too busy. We have to fill up every moment with words or sounds or activities. It seems like we are threatened by silence, by the freedom to just wait on the Lord for a word. But the song says, "Because I fear His Holy name, I will wait . . ." and "I will wait as long as it takes." I think the assembled people need to learn how to wait upon the Lord, for in worship God speaks.

I need to speak more fully to this concept that God speaks in worship. Many Christians mistakenly describe worship in terms of singing only. Singing is a very crucial part of worship, but it is not all we do in worship. In worship we also hear from God. First, we assemble, gather, and come together. And then God speaks and acts in the assembly.

There are many ways in which God speaks to us. God may speak to us through a song, a testimony, a word, or even the worship of another worshiper. But my concern here is to stress how God speaks to us through preaching. Let me give you an example.

A few years ago an elder at my church spoke at a Sunday evening service on the topic of having a childlike openness before God. He stressed how we come to God as our Father no matter how mature we grow in the faith and no matter how much responsibility we have been given. He said, "You might be a pastor, a worship leader, or even a bishop, but no matter what your ministry is, you're still a child of God."

I was just beginning my own ministry at that time. I was very young and sensing that bad things can happen to people who minister. I thought of how people put ministers on a pedestal and forget that they have weaknesses, too. As I meditated on that sermon, the song "The Warrior Is a Child" came to me. The song begins with these words:

Lately I've been winning battles left and right
But even winners can get wounded in the fight
People say that I'm amazing
Strong beyond my years
But they don't see inside of me
I'm hiding all the tears

They don't know
That I go running home when I fall down
They don't know
Who picks me up when no one is around
I drop my sword and cry for just a while
'Cause deep inside this armour
The warrior is a child

Unafraid because His armour is the best
But even soldiers need a quiet place to rest
People say that I'm amazing
Never face retreat
But they don't see the enemies
That lay me at His feet

They don't know
That I go running home when I fall down
They don't know
Who picks me up when no one is around
I drop my sword and cry for just a while
'Cause deep inside this armour
The warrior is a child

This song, more than any other song I've written, has generated response from ministers and Christian workers who tell me how much the song has ministered to them and encouraged them. Several ministers have actually told me that they were so discouraged and frustrated that they were thinking of quitting the ministry. But this song spoke to them, brought them healing, restoration of faith, and encouragement in ministry.

So, I thank the Lord for the Word of God that is faithfully preached. And, I thank the Lord that His Word does not return empty, but accomplishes His purposes in the lives of those who hear.

I often think, "What if I had not been in the church that night? What if I hadn't heard that sermon?" I've literally heard from thousands of people whose lives have been blessed by the song that was inspired by that sermon. This makes me realize how important preaching is. And how imperative it is that we be attentive to preaching. It might trigger something in us that will have a rippling effect and touch many lives.

DEVOTIONAL TEACHING

The second act of public worship centers around the Word of the Lord proclaimed and heard. The proclamation of the Word has been a major act of worship from the very beginning of the church. Luke tell us, for example, in Acts 2:46 that the primitive church gathered around the "apostolic teaching."

I like to imagine that the apostles frequently came through Jerusalem as part of their itinerant ministries and that preachers in training with the apostles were resident within Jerusalem and other cities.

The apostles were the authoritative interpreters of the Old Testament Scriptures and of the life, ministry, death, resurrection, and coming again of Jesus. They were also the storytellers, the ones who preserved the stories and acts of Jesus which were eventually collected in the Gospel writings and were then read and commented on in Christian worship.

This theme of "storytelling" is an important one for us to keep in mind. The Scripture is the story of Creation, of the Fall, of redemption, and of future hope. It is the story that is to be told, proclaimed, and explained in worship particularly in the service of the Word.

But there is a great danger of creating our own culturized version of this story. What we want in worship is a clear presentation of the gospel story as presented in the Scripture without the baggage of our own addition to the gospel. For it is the pure unadulterated Word of God that will awaken true faith. In this chapter we want to present the proclamation of the Word which is central to worship and help us grasp the effect it has on us when we proclaim it in its simplicity.

HEAR THE WORD OF THE LORD

I have always been taught that an essential feature of biblical religion is that it is a religion of the Word. The Word is that which is heard, acted upon, and obeyed. The phrase "Hear the Word of the Lord," which appears frequently in the prophetic literature of the Old Testament, is a statement that demands radical attention. The words that the prophets speak are not their own; they are the living, acting, powerful words of the Creator of heaven and earth, the sovereign Lord over all the affairs of humanity. The person who hears the Word of the Lord and decides to live in that Word is the one who "seeks the Lord." It is this Word that instructs Israel "to act justly and to love mercy and to walk humbly with your God" (Mic. 6:8). God's will is made known through the Word. Consequently, the failure of Israel is always related to their unwillingness to hear and to obey the Word of the Lord (see Amos 5:4-27).

In seminary I was taught that the emphasis on hearing and obeying the Word is carried through into the New Testament, which is likewise a revelation, a word to be heard. The New Testament is an announcement demanding a response. In this sense hearing becomes the technical term for the appropriation of the New Testament proclamation through which a person receives faith. The person who hears the proclamation about Christ is the one who has faith. As Paul wrote: "Consequently, faith comes from hearing the message, and the message is heard through the word of Christ" (Rom. 10:17).

I am convinced that the only mark by which one is able to distinguish true hearing from purely physical hearing is faith. Faith is the active affirmation of what is heard. The one who hears but does not hear simply makes a mental note of what has been heard but never really does anything about it. This person is described in James: "Anyone who listens to the word but does not do what it says is like a man who looks at his face in a mirror and, after looking at himself, goes away and immediately forgets what he looks like" (James 1:23-24). But the one who really hears is like the person who ". . . looks intently into the perfect law that gives freedom, and continues to do this, not forgetting what he has heard, but doing it— he will be blessed in what he does" (James 1:25). Hearing that is real hearing results in obedience to what was heard.

THE WORD WE LIVE BY

I don't think the starting point for hearing God is conceptual thought nor experience but the "word" we live by. By word I mean that truth by which we order our lives. The word we live by is the word we really hear and act upon. Let me explain.

All of us meet life on the level of daily human experience. Life is our constant companion. The extent to which we are forced to deal with the meaning of life is determined by the particular situations in which we find ourselves. For example, encounters with pain, sorrow, and death confront us with our "limitations" in an unusually forcible way. In this kind of a situation, only an extraordinarily insensitive person will not think deeply about the meaning of life.

More common, however, are the less dramatic, somewhat humdrum activities of life that confront us every day. Our daily decision-making process is based on our underlying assumptions about life. Our decisions about behavior, thoughts, and opinions, always relate to the word we live by.

Whether we know it or not, each of us is a product of our time. We are the way we are in part because of the people who have influenced us, the books we have read, the television shows we have seen, the places we have gone, and the things we think about. The twentieth century has contributed to the shaping of our lives: its sights and sounds, wars and crime, noise and pollution, and varieties of ideologies. What we have been, what we are, what we will be are all related to these forces that close in on us and demand our response. Each of these forces represents a word, a voice, that asks us to hear what it says and to act upon what we've heard!

The word we hear and live by is the word we worship. Think of all the words that demand our response.

The word of humanism proclaims, "Man is the measure of all things." It calls us to make man our god and to worship and serve the creature rather than the Creator. The word of determinism announces that a person is nothing more than a cork on the ocean of life, tossed to and fro by the forces of life. The word of materialism tempts us to live as though matter alone is the true basis for life. We are to make the almighty dollar our goal, our highest value in life. The word of relativism announces that truth varies from person to person. Everyone makes his/her own rules and lives according to his/her own liking. The word of the organization man is to "climb the ladder," "be the person on the top." The word of complacency gives top priority to the establishment and to "security." The word of despair proclaims the ultimate meaninglessness of life, a journey from nothing to nothing. And there are more words—technocrat, compartmentalization, neurotic, ad infinitum.

These words, which represent an entire way of thinking of life, press in on us every day demanding us to hear and live by them. The word we live by is the word we worship.

Now let's look at hearing from another point of view. There is another word that has entered into life, demanding our attention, our response. It is that Word of God embodied in Jesus Christ.

> In the beginning was the Word, and the Word was with God, and the Word was God. (John 1:1) The Word became flesh and made his dwelling among us. We have seen his glory, the glory of the One and Only, who came from the Father, full of grace and truth. (John 1:14)

The Center of the universe, the One from whom all things derive life and meaning, stepped into human history. He has proclaimed His presence. He has announced His lordship over all of life. He calls us to hear Him and to live by His Word. The person who hears the Word of the Lord Christ and lives according to it lives out of the context of a biblical worldview. Faith has been awakened.

TRUE HEARING—AWARENESS AND OBEDIENCE

I believe that when we truly hear the Word of the Lord in worship, we respond with awareness and obedience.

Awareness is that quality of hearing that results in the inner sense of the presence of God. It is an ongoing encounter with the reality that God is there. Such awareness goes deeper than experience, although we are able to "feel" the experience to a certain degree. Rather, spiritual awareness lets us in on something higher and more powerful, something deeper and more sublime than words can convey or experiences can reveal. It expresses itself in a sense of wonder, amazement, awe, and renewed sensitivity to life.

When the Word of the Lord in Christ is truly heard in worship, there is a response deep down in the inner person that says, "Yes, what I have heard is the truth about life. I am willing to risk my life that it is true. This is the Word by which I will allow my life to be shaped." Paul testified to this awareness: "Because you are sons, God sent the Spirit of his Son into our hearts, the Spirit who calls out, 'Abba, Father'" (Gal. 4:6).

The awareness of God and our relation to Him and to His world results in the desire to obey. It is at this point where the concept of the word we live by becomes apparent. The Christian worldview is shaped in obedience to the Word. The Christian takes the Word seriously. A Christian worships the living Word, Jesus Christ. That means a Christian will do anything the Word commands. A Christian will construct a philosophy about life according to the Word; a Christian will eat, sleep, and drink in the presence of the Word. In the struggle between the Word and words, a Christian will consciously seek to say "yes" to the Word and "no" to all other words. A Christian will live by the living Word that is proclaimed through the pages of the written Word. A Christian's ultimate concern in life will be to serve the Word, the King, the Lord of life, and humanity. This is what it means to worship the Word; obedience to the Word becomes our work, our response to God.

In my own experience of worship, I am continually driven back into the Hebraic worldview. Here we find a correlation between faith and hearing. To hear something is to live by it. Thus, our calling and service of the Word is not merely to accept the content of faith, nor is it to have evoked within us some warm and tender feelings about Christ. Rather, the point of the service of the Word is to awaken faith and incite obedience.

Christian faith finds expression in terms of awareness and obedience. Awareness affects the mind. It creates a new orientation toward life: the believer perceives reality from the perspective of the Incarnation, the redemption, and the re-creation of all things. On the other hand, obedience affects the life: the Christian gains a new set of values, new goals, and new purposes. This is what the Christian gains in worship through the hearing of the Word: awareness and obedience.

The issue of worship is therefore related to all of life. Since Christ is Lord of the whole creation, the reorientation of our lives through the hearing of the Word is the goal of the service of the Word.

CHALLENGE

The challenge for the church and its leadership is to give Scripture reading and preaching a place of central importance in worship.

The ancient liturgy of the church, drawing from the synagogue, placed a high priority on the Word read and spoken. Reading and preaching, properly understood are an art. Reading and preaching intend to recreate. It is not a mere "dead" reading or preaching. Consequently, we ought to do much more in our churches to improve the ability of communication through reading the Scripture and preaching. Our reading and preaching needs to be a proclamation.

A proclamation is more like an announcement than a treatise and should be expressed with a sense of urgency, clarity, and precision. Thus scriptural proclamation ought to be characterized by dynamic power and not be a mere statement of fact. It is a lively Word: a "word that goes out from my mouth: It will not return to me empty, but will accomplish what I desire and achieve the purpose for which I sent it" (Isa. 55:11). Much liturgical reading of the Word is characterized by dullness. Too much of our preaching sounds like a moral diatribe or an outdated lecture. Reading and preaching, properly executed, can trigger the imagination and create visual images, thus communicating the reality they present.

And, of course, the second challenge is to learn how to hear. "He who has ears, let him hear" (Matt. 11:15) is an admonition directed to us today. We live in a world of words, and too often we conveniently turn down the sound and stop listening. We must recover the art of hearing—and of acting on what we have heard.

CHAPTER EIGHT

Giving Thanks
"At the Lord's Supper we give thanks for Christ's
sacrifice on the cross."

Your only Son, no sin to hide
But You have sent Him from Your side
To walk upon this guilty sod
And to become the Lamb of God

Your gift of Love they crucified
They laughed and scorned Him as He died
The humble King they named a fraud
And sacrificed the Lamb of God

O Lamb of God, sweet Lamb of God
I love the Holy Lamb of God
O wash me in His precious blood
My Jesus Christ, the Lamb of God

I was so lost, I should have died
But You have brought me to Your side
To be led by Your staff and rod
And to be called a lamb of God

O Lamb of God, sweet Lamb of God
I love the Holy Lamb of God
O wash me in His precious blood
'Til I am just a lamb of God
O wash me in His precious blood
My Jesus Christ, the Lamb of God

("LAMB OF GOD")

INTERPRETATION

Over the past few years, God has been working in my heart and expanding my understanding of worship. Because we think of God as a spirit, we often interpret our worship to be the communion of our spirit with God's Spirit. But lately, God has been impressing upon me that God did not come to this earth as a spirit, but as flesh and blood.

When I think of the Incarnation, I am struck with the earthiness, the tangible, physical nature of Christianity. Think of it! God, the creator of the material world, actually becoming the material world. He became one of us so that He could represent us in our flesh and blood to the Father.

I think this theme is captured in my song "Lamb of God," especially in the phrase, "To walk upon this guilty sod and to become the Lamb of God." This song captures the physical, tangible side of the Christian faith. Words such as "crucified," "laughed," "scorned," "sacrificed," are words of a physical reality. Even the words of the chorus such as "wash me in His precious blood," "brought me to your side," and "led by your staff and rod" connote the physical side of our spirituality.

In worship this physical side of our spirituality is expressed in communion. Recently I've become aware of how deeply committed New Testament Christians were to eating the bread and drinking the wine as a powerful spiritual act of remembering the death and resurrection of Jesus Christ.

I've learned that the remembering we do focuses on the victory Christ has obtained over the powers of evil. This is not only a victory accomplished at the Cross, but one that is continually accomplished in our lives in worship.

This concept of God's victory over the enemies of God, the powers of evil, the victory which we celebrate at communion is expressed in my song "The Battle Is the Lord's." In this song I sing of how God will "conquer all His enemies, with His right hand, and

His only arm, and He will obtain the victory. The princes of the earth and of the sky shall see His holy power." In communion we actually experience this power of the Lord through the symbols of bread and wine, so our response is to "break forth and sing for joy, sing praises to the Lord, for He is coming, He is coming." When God comes, God will put away the powers of evil forever and create a new heaven and a new earth where there will be no more evil, no more pain and sorrow. So communion not only looks back to the victory accomplished in the death of Christ, but forward to the victory of Christ over evil at the end of history.

Another aspect of communion that I'm learning about is that when we pray and give thanks over the bread and wine, we commemorate all of God's saving work from the beginning of time, a work of salvation that culminates in the work of Christ. I think I capture this praise for the history of God's saving work in my song "You Have Been Good." The song says, "You have been faithful to all generations, Oh Lord, your steadfast love and tender mercy have been our salvation . . . for by our hand we have been led and by your spirit we have been led." In communion we recite God's saving deeds in history, and we respond in praise and adoration. For this reason I feel most at home in a communion that is not like a sober funeral dirge, but a communion that is full of life and song. Many worshiping communities now sing songs of resurrection and exaltation as people are receiving communion. I like this because it allows me to commemorate God's saving work for me as I participate in the symbols of salvation — the bread and wine.

DEVOTIONAL TEACHING

Not long ago a minister from North Carolina called me to tell me about the renewal of worship in his congregation and the powerful effect this renewal had on the lives of his people.

After he had finished telling me the story of renewal, I asked, "Where did all of this start? What was the first thing you did?"

Without a moment's hesitation the pastor answered, "Our renewal began when we focused on the Lord's Supper. It was here that the lives of people were changed."

The third act of Christian worship is one that has been neglected in many churches today. It is the specific act of remembering, enacting, and celebrating the living, dying, and rising of Christ through symbols of bread and wine.

I want to begin our study of the Lord's Table by focusing on the four terms used in the New Testament to describe our worship at the Table of the Lord.

FOUR NEW TESTAMENT TERMS FOR THE TABLE OF THE LORD

The oldest term for what we do at the Table of the Lord is breaking bread, which is found in Acts 2:42: "They devoted themselves to the apostles' teaching and to the fellowship, to the breaking of bread and to prayer." This term has as its particular point of reference the presence of the resurrected Lord in the midst of the worshiping community. This experience of the resurrected presence of Jesus at His Table is based on the presence of Jesus in eating on the Emmaus road (Luke 24:13-32); in the Upper Room (Luke 24:36-49); and by the Sea of Galilee (John 21:1-14). In each of these instances, Jesus was recognized by the disciples in the breaking of the bread (Luke 24:35). Consequently, when the early Christians broke bread in their homes, they expected and experienced the presence of the resurrected Christ. Jesus "shows up" when we break bread at His Table.

A second term, the Lord's Supper, is used by Paul in 1 Corinthians 11:20. Paul used the term as a corrective to the misuse of the love feast, the name of the primitive service of bread breaking. Apparently some of the new Corinthian believers were celebrating the resurrection too much and were becoming drunk. Therefore, Paul reminded them that the feast of the Lord was also a remembrance of the death of Jesus by quoting the words of Jesus "and when he had given thanks, he broke it and said, 'This is my body, which is for you; do this in remembrance of me'" (1 Cor. 11:24).

The third term for the Table of the Lord is communion, a term based on 1 Corinthians 10:16: "Is not the cup of thanksgiving for which we give thanks a participation in the blood of Christ? And is not the bread that we break a participation in the body of Christ?" This term "participation" which is also translated "communion" speaks to the mystery of our participation in the body and blood of the Lord. Christians through the centuries have attached various meanings to this participation, ranging from the designation of transubstantiation (the bread and wine are turned into the body and blood and ingested) to the denial of the presence of the Lord at bread and wine in the doctrine of memorialism (we remember the death in our minds). Many now recognize these two assertions to be at the two extremes of a spectrum, and repudiating both, opt for an assertion of the mystery of Christ's presence at the table of the Lord through terms such as "real presence" or "manifest presence."

The final term, Eucharist, also appears in the Pauline literature. When Paul is admonishing the Corinthian Christians about the use of tongues in worship, he says: "If you are praising God with your spirit, how can one who finds himself among those who do not understand say 'Amen' to your thanksgiving [Eucharist], since he does not know what you are saying?" (1 Cor. 14:16).

This term "Eucharist" simply means to make thanks and has been used throughout history to refer to the church's prayer of thanksgiving which is said over the bread and wine for the death and resurrection of Christ and the benefit of salvation.

These four terms then give us the larger picture of what happens at the Table of the Lord. In sum, the Table of the Lord is a symbolic act of remembrance in which the risen Christ becomes present to do for us what He did for us on the cross. And we give thanks. We need to recover this central symbol of worship and symbolism in general because symbolism is a powerful way to communicate Christ in worship. Let me explain.

THE PLACE OF SYMBOLISM IN WORSHIP

It is generally recognized that a symbol both points beyond itself and participates in that which it symbolizes. For example, the American flag is a symbol because it both represents the United States of America and because it actually participates in the reality it presents. That is, the American flag is a piece of America. The same can be said of the symbols of bread and wine. They represent Jesus. But more than that, bread and wine participate in the reality they represent. In worship they are the manifest presence of Jesus. They symbolize His saving and healing power.

THE SIGNIFICANCE OF SYMBOLS

When we consider the function of symbols as a means of understanding and communicating the Christian faith, we must not treat them as mere psychological creations but as images of an ultimate reality. The realm of the supernatural is as real as the natural. Thus, a symbol in the natural world corresponds to a reality of the supernatural world. The church in the world corresponds to the church in the mind of God. The bread and wine in the church corresponds to the body and blood of Christ broken and shed for our salvation.

THE NECESSITY OF SYMBOLIC COMMUNICATION

The nature of faith itself demands the transformation of supernatural concepts into visible images and symbols. Because no finite language can fully and completely express supernatural truth adequately, biblical religion and the church in history have always relied on symbolism as a means of communicating that which transcends the realm of the finite. The language of faith has always, therefore, been a language of symbols such as bread, wine, water, and oil.

A glance at the history of worship suggests that it has only been in modern history, and especially within the Protestant Christian community, that symbolic communication has fallen into disuse. The rise of the printed page in the sixteenth century replaced the ancient symbolism of worship with the written word. The chief form of communication in the West has been reading and writing. The invention of radio, however, signaled a shift toward the recovery of other senses in communication. Sensory communication has accelerated with the introduction of television and new advertising techniques. As people become more and more dependent on a visual means of communication, reading and writing skills will go into decline, and the impact of the visual will assume greater proportions. This means it is particularly important for the church to recapture once again the use of symbolism as a means of communication. This is especially important for Protestants, whose reform was sparked and spread by the revolution introduced by the Gutenberg press.

In my own experience, I have become aware of the lack of symbolism in Protestant worship. We Protestants are accustomed to simple and straightforward language. The use of imagery, symbols, and even subtle language is relatively unknown among many of us because we have locked ourselves into speech as the preferable, if not the only, form of communication.

I think one reason why we Evangelicals prefer verbal communication over symbolic communication has to do with our view of the Bible. We see the Bible as a Book of words. It is God's written revelation. This emphasis on the written words of Scripture coupled with an attitude of neglect toward the symbolic forms of communication (which constitute a large portion of Scripture) have caused us to lose the significance of the symbolic in worship.

Another reason why we use words as the major means of communication is found in our strong sense of persons as reasonable creatures. Today a strong emphasis is placed on the mind. Because people above all other creatures are rational, they are able to investigate the words of Scripture and seek from them the correct meaning of things. Therefore, the emphasis falls on words and cognitive understanding in Protestant worship.

We have to remember that while words play an important part in communication, there is nevertheless another dimension of communication that needs further exploration — symbolism. Symbolic communication is affirmed in the Scriptures. Scripture is filled with visions, dreams, imagery, and apocalyptic material. Furthermore, the assumption that people are predominately verbal creatures greatly underestimates the imaginative side of humanity.

We should recover symbolism because we are symbolic creatures. For example, recent research in psychology, especially that branch which attempts to understand the neural organization of the human mind, has concluded that our brain functions differently in the right and left hemispheres. The left hemisphere appears to specialize in verbal functions, and the right hemisphere centers on spatial functions and other nonverbal skills.

These facts should influence us to think about the importance of symbolism in worship. Stephen G. Meyer, in an article entitled "Neuropsychology and Worship," helps us discover the power of the symbolic in worship. His argument, which begins with Scripture, is that (1) while Scripture is verbal, the material it communicates is based on a variety of communication models, ranging from discursive expression to highly apocalyptic language to poetic discourse; (2) although Christianity is grounded on reason, illustrated by Paul's reasoning from the Scriptures in the synagogue (see Acts 17:2) or Peter's insisting that Christians give "an answer to everyone who asks you to give the reason for the hope that you have . . . " (1 Pet. 3:15), there are nevertheless "definitive confrontations between God and man where there is concurrent use of vision and word." Meyer cites the examples of Ezekiel, Job, and John (Revelation) and concludes that "while the Bible presents the Christian faith as a rational faith, the rationale is built on symbols which outline its structure" (Stephen G. Meyer, "Neuropsychology and Worship" *Journal of Psychology and Theology*, (Fall, 1975), pp. 281-289).

Rollo May argues that the loss of symbols constitutes one of our chief difficulties. When we have no symbols to identify and illustrate the meaning of life, we are not able to transcend the crises of life. Hunger, war, death, unemployment, disease, and the other horrors that confront us on a daily basis seem to be the sum and substance of life. Without signs or symbols in this world to show us another world or a means of coping with the trials and strains of this world, we have nowhere to turn but to despair and absurdity.

Also, we should recover the use of symbolism because symbolism is at the very center of life itself. In celebrations such as birthdays, anniversaries, graduations, marriages, funerals, and the like we act out the meaning of things that words alone fail to convey.

Likewise, the great drama of the world as expressed in Scripture, ought to be communicated in worship not only in words but in the actions of the church. Symbolic communication in worship is a valid means of communicating truths of the Christian faith. The reenactment of the birth of Christ, the sorrow over His death, the joy of His resurrection, and the power of Pentecost cannot be completely or adequately communicated through words alone. If our brain is oriented toward spatial as well as verbal communication, then Christian worship must not neglect the symbolic and nonverbal means of communication.

CHALLENGE

Our challenge is to recover that sense in which the truth of the Christian message may be expressed through the art of rehearsal. Symbolic rehearsal is the dramatic re-creation of God's saving events. At the Lord's Table we rehearse and represent the great events of redemptive history, the dying and rising of Christ.

The origin of dramatic representation in worship is found in the Old Testament experience of the Passover and other festivals.

Even as the Passover is the rehearsal of the Exodus Event, so the Christian Eucharist rehearses the Christ Event.

In this event dramatized, through the symbols of bread and wine, the God of history is made present in a visible and tangible way, proclaiming His saving work through the senses of sight, touch, smell, and taste.

At the Table of the Lord we remember that all-important event which saves us from our sin and frees us from the power of the evil one. Furthermore, bread and wine point to the future for it proclaims the death of Christ "till he comes" (1 Cor. 11:26). It lifts us out of the mundane and speaks to us of the ultimate meaning of life. It says that this world is not all that is, that our ultimate destiny is in the new heaven and the new earth.

By the same token, the symbols of bread and wine do not deny the reality of this world. Rather, by bringing the past and the future together, the bread and wine communicate the meaning of history and of our place in it. It, therefore, sends us forth into the world to be a continuing agent of God's reconciliation to the world. This is the hope that has been expressed in the symbol of the redeemed community, the church, especially in its worship at the Table of the Lord.

What of the future? How are we to view the changes occurring in communications in the twentieth century? How should these changes affect our approach to worship? A single point will suffice:

the communication of the Christian message in worship must be directed toward the imaginative as well as the cognitive level of the worshiper. This is a legitimate field into which the church may enter. Involvement in visual communication is rooted in the biblical tradition. Our challenge has to do with the future of worship as it relates to the recovery of biblical worship and to the changing forms of communication in an audio-visual society. It is, I believe, imperative for us to recover the regular celebration of the symbols of Christ's victory over the powers of evil at the Table of the Lord not only because the Bible teaches it, but because we are in great need of the hope delivered by the symbols of bread and wine.

CHAPTER NINE

Going Forth
"The final act of corporate worship is a benediction,
a blessing, a charge laid upon our lives as we go forth into
the world where our service of the Lord continues."

I am ready to be
All You've given me to be
Lord I offer You my pride
Lay it down
Where I have been bound
Father come and set me free
I am ready now to be finally — me

I am ready to be
All You've given me to be
Lord I offer You my life
Lay it down
Where I have been bound
Father come and set me free
I am ready now to be
Finally, faithfully, willingly — me

("I AM READY")

INTERPRETATION

We all know that worship is not only what we do when we
assemble together, but also what we do when we scatter into the world.

"I Am Ready" is a song that expresses our going forth into the
world to love and serve the Lord. This is one of those songs that just

came to me out of my heart while I was responding to what God was doing in my life. Let me explain.

I'm really a "comfort zone clinger." I mean I like to settle down in my nest, know the parameters of my life, have everything neatly organized and secure. I don't like to get pushed out of my comfort zones.

This song resulted from a particular time in my life when God was nudging me out of my comfort zone, pushing me out of my nest. Like a lot of people, I'm not anxious to move out into the cruel and unknown world. But God was prompting me to move out. I wasn't sure that I had the gifts or talents to do what God was asking, so in my heart I was going through some resistance. But later, when I yielded to God, I knew that God would go with me. I was ready to be the person God wanted me to be, and I knew God could give me the grace and ability to do what He was calling me to do.

A worship dismissal charges us to go forth into the world to be who God wants us to be and to do what God wants us to do. Our response to God's sending us should be to say, "Lord, I want to do what You're asking me to do, and I don't want to hold back anymore."

I need to hear myself say those words because I've had a tendency to hold my arms in close and protect myself. But I know the only protection is God. I know it's silly to hold back and be afraid of anything God wants of me. And when I finally make the decision to be obedient to God and say "I'll do anything you want me to do," suddenly I'm no longer afraid. But refusing to do what God wants feeds the fear. It's the opposite of what you would expect. Doing God's will is a release. When I decided to do what God wanted me to do, it was like driving a stake into the ground. My choice to follow God was a marker, a decision, a commitment.

I think going forth from worship relates to our sense of mission in the world, to our commitment to evangelism and to our commitment to spiritual warfare. We, the body of Christ, are an extension of Jesus in the world.

The song "How Beautiful" reflects on our mission to the world, particularly in the phrase "How beautiful the hands that serve the wine and the bread and the sons of the earth." I'm not sure that everyone understands it this way, but the lyric is meant to express the concept that we are to be the reflection of Christ, that we are to do exactly what Christ did when He was here on earth. We are those people that the world can look at and say, "Look at the way they live, how they relate to each other, how much they love each other." Hopefully, because of our lives in this world, they can see that Christianity is real and not just walk away from it and dismiss it as unreal.

I also capture the sense of going forth from worship to serve the Lord in my song "Runner." Here I speak of the runner as "courier, valiant, bearing the flame, messenger noble, sent in His name, faster and harder, run through the night, desperate relay, carry the light, carry the light."

Worship sends us forth to carry the light. "Runner" was partly inspired by my relationship with Youth with a Mission. I think worship sends all of us forth as missionaries. We are to be true followers of Christ whether it's in our daily work, school settings, the home, or in an overseas setting.

I like to think of our service to God like a relay race, an image which I express in the phrase "mindful of many waiting to run." This refers to the younger believers, children, even those not yet born, who will pick up the baton and keep running. For centuries our forefathers and mothers have been running with the baton of the gospel. And they have passed it on from generation to generation, and now we have received the baton and will pass it on to our children. Someday this job will be done. Someday the baton will be passed for the last time, and our work in this world will come to an end. Worship looks to that end and empowers our running.

Several of my songs express what we do from now until the coming of Christ when our running will be finished. First, there is the song "I See You Standing." I was inspired to write this song when Michael Chang won the French Open in 1990. After he won and thanked all the people, he added, "Most of all I'd like to thank my Lord Jesus Christ without whom I'd be nothing."

My husband and I had been watching the tournament and had been cheering him on. We liked him, his approach to the game, and his whole demeanor. But we didn't know he was a Christian. When he said those words, I jumped out of my chair and shouted, "Yes!" I was so excited because he seized the moment to give glory to the Lord and to testify to his faith in a gracious and unpretentious way that wasn't offensive but drew people in to glorify Christ.

I wrote "I See You Standing" partly in response to Michael Chang's testimony. The chorus captures the moment: "I see you standing in the fire, standing on the Word, remembering the call. I see you standing, standing, I see you standing tall." I want to be like Michael Chang and stand!

I know most Christians want to serve the Lord and to be empowered to stand by their experience of worship. The song "Keeper of the Door" expresses my own struggle to know how God wants me to stand.

The song is my own story. It begins "I dreamed I saw my name in lights. I spoke your Word for all to hear." Those words address the temptation that any of us in public ministry feel from time to time. Those of us in the public eye walk a fine line. Recognition and applause can quickly appeal to the ego in the wrong way. I remember, as a young person, how I longed to be involved in Christian music but for all the wrong reasons. I wanted to experience the fun of singing, to be up on stage, and be the center of attention. I'd go to concerts and say, "Oh, I want to do that!"

Then the Lord took me through a process of growth over several years while I was in the Discipleship Training School in YWAM. God showed me that my ambitions, my dreams, my desires, and my goals had not been laid at the foot of the cross. I had not said, "Not my will but Your will be done." Those words can be an awfully difficult thing to say and mean. It's a lot harder to mean it than it is to say it.

But during Discipleship Training School, God was doing a lot of "heart surgery" on me. I came to the place of wanting to serve God in the way that He wanted me to, no matter what that meant. And even though I loved music, I was able to say, "You gave me this gift, and I lay this gift back down at Your feet. If You want me to go to Africa and clean bathrooms on a missionary compound, then I will do it and never play another note in my life." I even told my dad at one point, "I don't think the Lord is going to use my music. Certainly not on a large scale." I now realize that in order to know that you have given over your talent to God, you have to come to the place where you believe God is in complete control of your life.

It was not long after I gave my talent over to the Lord that the Lord suddenly began opening doors. God has this way of making things very clear. There were doors that I couldn't beat down before, but suddenly they were flying open because I had come to the place of ministry for the right motive—to serve God and the body.

I think all these things are related to worship, for worship empowers us to serve.

DEVOTIONAL TEACHING

Twila has touched on a very important aspect of worship by commenting on the fact that worship does not end at the door of the church but continues into all of life.

The final act of worship, the dismissal or the going forth as the title of the chapter says, is no mere "goodbye, I'll see you later." It's a benediction, a blessing, a charge laid upon our lives as we go forth into the world where our service of the Lord continues.

The Greek word *Leiturgia,* which is the word from which the word for worship ultimately derives, is literally translated as work. When we assemble for worship, the worship or the work of the people is to remember God's saving deeds and to give thanks. When we go forth from our assembled work, there is another dimension of worship or work we do which is the service of God in all of life. Paul speaks to this work when he writes, "Therefore, I urge you, brothers, in view of God's mercy, to offer your bodies as living sacrifices, holy and pleasing to God—this is your spiritual act of worship" (Rom. 12:1).

I want to explore our worship at work in the world, and I will do so from the perspective of the corporate church continuing its work of worship in the world. In this corporate work we take our place as individuals. Let's understand the work of worship in the world through the biblical themes that the church is not of the spirit of the world and that the church in Christ is victorious over the world.

THE CHURCH IS NOT OF THE SPIRIT OF THE WORLD

Both Paul and John speak of the world in a personified way. The world is the great enemy of Christ. It is the world that "did not recognize him" (John 1:10), it is the world of "rulers," "authorities," "the powers of this dark world," "spiritual forces of evil in the heavenly realms" (Eph. 6:12). This is the world that hates Christ as He Himself said: "The world cannot hate you, but it hates me because I testify that what it does is evil" (John 7:7). The world also hates the church because, as Jesus said, "If you belonged to the world, it would love you as its own. As it is, you do not belong to the world, but I have chosen you out of the world. That is why the world hates you" (John 15:19).

This world, the world of evil powers, greed, hate, violence, lust, immorality, murder, is the world Christ has judged. To the crowd that came to hear Him after they had heard of His raising Lazarus from the dead, Jesus said, "Now is the time for judgment on this world; now the prince of this world will be driven out" (John 12:31, cf. John 14:30; 16:11). Paul, interpreting Christ's death, wrote, "And having disarmed the powers and authorities, he made a public spectacle of them, triumphing over them by the cross" (Col. 2:15).

The stance of the worshiping church toward the world is, therefore, quite clear. Paul wrote, "Do not conform any longer to the pattern of this world . . ." (Rom. 12:2). He urged the church to recognize "this world in its present form is passing away" (1 Cor. 7:31). James also reminded the Christians ". . . don't you know that friendship with the world is hatred toward God?" (James 4:4). John is no less clear, cautioning the church to "not love the world or anything in the world. If anyone loves the world, the love of the Father is not in him" (1 John 2:15).

It is clear from the teaching of the New Testament that the worshiping church is called to take an active stance against the world, against the powers of evil. The question is: how does the church communicate its stance against the powers?

In the first place, the worshiping church is called to fulfill the Great Commission (Acts 1:8; Matt. 28:19). It is the church's responsibility to preach the word of reconciliation, to declare Christ's victory over evil, and to invite people to renounce their allegiance to sin and to follow Jesus in His church.

This commission cannot be replaced or fall into disuse. It is still the primary means of spreading the gospel. Our concern for Christian architecture, music, art, and literature dare not replace the significance of personal witness to the power of Christ. Because worship continually rehearses God's work of salvation, worship empowers us to witness to the saving power of Jesus Christ.

Second, because worship celebrates the confrontation of the powers by Christ, it should shape our life into a prophetic stance. The prophet calls for an application of the Word of God to the very life-structure of society. The prophetic voice challenges the permeation of evil in society and its expression within the institutions of society. Like Amos, the prophetic voice calls: "But let justice roll on like a river, righteousness like a never-failing stream!" (Amos 5:24).

The prophetic stance is not only a voice but also an alternative lifestyle. The worshiping church is called to live in such a way that it expresses its freedom from worldly domination and bondage. It is an organism of people expressing a new fabric of human relationships, modeled on a commitment to a lifestyle that sharply contrasts with the world's. Its power is the power of service, not of domination.

A third way the worshiping church speaks against the world is in its formation of values. Worship, particularly baptism and preaching, calls for the worshiping person to live by the moral teachings of Jesus.

For example, in Romans 6, the great baptismal passages of the New Testament, Paul wrote, "Don't you know that when you offer yourselves to someone to obey him as slaves, you are slaves to the one whom you obey—whether you are slaves to sin, which leads to death, or to obedience, which leads to righteousness?" (Rom. 6:16). Paul spelled out the worshiper's baptismal values in a catalogue of sins in Galatians and Colossians. He said the baptized person will avoid the "sinful nature" and listed "sexual immorality, impurity and debauchery; idolatry and witchcraft; hatred, discord, jealousy, fits of rage, selfish ambition, dissensions, factions and envy; drunkenness, orgies, and the like . . ." (Gal. 5:19-21). To the Colossians he cited similar evils and then called on these Christians to put away "anger, rage, malice, slander, and filthy language from your lips" (Col. 3:8). The worshiping person learns to put off these sins of the flesh and to rise to a new life characterized by the fruits of the Spirit, which are: "love, joy, peace, patience, kindness, goodness, faithfulness, gentleness and self-control" (Gal. 5:22-23). Baptismal worship shapes us into the kind of person that continually puts away evil and continually puts on Christ.

The Church in Christ Is Victorious Over the World

A second relationship the worshiping church sustains with the world is proclaimed in the preaching and teaching of Jesus that He has overcome evil powers. He said to His disciples, ". . . In this world you will have trouble. But take heart! I have overcome the world" (John 16:33). Paul interpreted Christ's death as a victory over the powers of evil. "And having disarmed the powers and authorities, he made a public spectacle of them, triumphing over them by the cross" (Col. 2:15).

Because Christ is victorious over the world, the church, which is the body of Christ, is called to exercise Christ's victory over the world now.

The first and most obvious means of communicating the victory of Christ over evil is through preaching. Paul stressed the importance of preaching in his letter to the Romans. "How, then, can they call on the one they have not believed in? And how can they believe in the one of whom they have not heard? And how can they hear without someone preaching to them?" (Rom. 10:14).

The word preach does not mean to explain or moralize but to announce and proclaim. The church has a joyful announcement to make to the world—humanity and the created order have been released from the power of sin and set free (Rom. 6:6, 8).

A major problem with preaching today is a failure to see preaching as a message of victory and to see the method of proclaiming this victory as an announcement. When we garble the message of Christ into a mere belief system or a calling to moral awareness, the message lacks its power.

Next, if we want to live lives that experience the victory of Christ over the powers of evil, we must be open to the ministry of the Holy Spirit in our worship, especially at the Lord's Table.

In the ancient church Christ's victory over sin was proclaimed at the Lord's Table and experienced in eating the bread and drinking the wine. Ignatius (A.D. 110) wrote to the Ephesians, commending them to "break one loaf, which is the medicine of immortality, and the antidote which wards off death but yields continuous life in union with Jesus Christ."

If we regard the Lord's Supper as a mere memorial and nothing else, we cut ourselves off from the immediate benefit of receiving the very life and power of Jesus. At the Table of the Lord we encounter Jesus, and through His power, healing is given to our whole person.

A good example of communicating Christ's victory over evil at the Table of the Lord is found in the life and ministry of John of Kronstadt, a nineteenth-century priest in Russia. He was a man of prayer, and his chief contribution to the Russian church was in connection with the profound, mystical, living experience of the Eucharist. In the Orthodox church no one is allowed to take Communion until he or she has confessed their sins to the priest. Since, in a large congregation, this practice inhibits frequent Communion, Father Kronstadt introduced the unheard of practice of general vocal confession. It was, as George Fedotov wrote, "an impressive, even terrifying spectacle: Thousands of people shouting aloud their most secret sins and sobbing for forgiveness."

Father Kronstadt records how the experience of confession and the reception of the symbols of bread and wine resulted in physical and emotional healings and how his congregation became empowered in their spiritual lives, attaining victory over the powers of evil.

The victory of Christ over evil has the effect of transforming us and our world. This transformation is primarily a transformation of the Christian community, the church, which in turn radiates the message of redemption and reconciliation to the entire created order. The church is, therefore, called to be the recipient of the redeeming work of Christ and to be the source for the redeeming presence of Christ in the world. Thus, Christ communicates Himself to the church, and the church communicates Christ to the world.

CHALLENGE

The challenge of this chapter is to understand the role of the worshiping church as communicator of Christ to the world. In America, and among Protestants in particular, we usually think of one-to-one interpersonal communication or electronic mass communication. We seldom think in terms of the communication made by the mere presence of a group in society. This tendency needs correction, because it disregards the total impact a unified body can make on society. This one-sided view of communication tends to make one see the church as a collection of individuals rather than the body of Christ. By returning to the more corporate sense of the church, our understanding of going from worship takes on a new dimension, an added depth.

Our challenge is to recognize that the worshiping church communicates to the world (i.e., the powers of evil) by shaping a society of people who live over against the powers. The powers and all their influence have been decisively defeated in the death and resurrection of Christ. The worshiping church, therefore, as the community of those being released from the powers of evil and formed into a new people by the story enacted in worship, go into the world to provide healing in the power of the Holy Spirit.

Chapter Ten

Nurturing Faith Through Worship
"It is in the context of the church at worship
that spiritual growth takes place."

For the young abandoned husband
Left alone without a reason
For the pilgrim in the city where there is no home
For the son without a father
For his solitary mother
I have a message
He sees you. He knows you
He loves you. He loves you

Every heart that is breaking tonight
Is the heart of a child that He holds in His sight
And oh how He longs to hold in His arms
Every heart that is breaking tonight

For the precious, fallen daughter
For her devastated father
For the prodigal who's dying in a strange new way
For the child who's always hungry
For the patriot with no country
I have a message
He sees you. He knows you
He loves you. Jesus loves you

Every heart that is breaking tonight
Is the heart of a child that He holds in His sight
And oh how He longs to hold in His arms
Every heart that is breaking tonight

("Every Heart That Is Breaking")

INTERPRETATION

My husband, Jack, has a good friend from college who got married shortly after we did. They keep up with each other as friends by going to dinner together every once in a while.

One night Jack's friend called and asked Jack to go to lunch with him the next day. Jack thought he sounded down in his spirits, but didn't press him about it on the phone, figuring if there was something wrong he would hear of it the next day.

Unfortunately, the news was not good. Before a year had gone by in the marriage, his bride decided she did not love him and had simply packed up and left him without notice or reason.

Being a newlywed myself, I was sickened by the tragic circumstances of Jack's friend. That night my sleep was restless and full of pain, so I got up, went alone into my music room, and in the early hours of the morning, I continued to think about the pain he was going through.

As I sat there meditating on his pain, I began to see the heart of God as it was turned toward Jack's friend and all the hurting people of the world. I know that God is fully aware of all the suffering people go through and that God can bring comfort and healing to their lives.

I began to think of different examples of hurting people, and the song "Every Heart That Is Breaking" came to me. For every line in that song I have a personal example: the mother and young boy who had recently lost a father, the fallen teenager and her devastated father, the son dying with AIDS, the hungry child, and the refugee. For them the message is that God sees you, and knows you, and loves you.

I think worship ministers to the hurting people of the world because God is present in worship to bring a healing touch into our lives. A lot of people say, "Don't go to worship to get, go to worship to give." I think that's a half-truth.

We do go to worship to give glory and honor to God. But worship is a two-way action. God is there doing what God has done for us in Jesus Christ. In Christ, God conquered all the powers of evil and will ultimately, through the death and resurrection of Christ, bring healing to all the nations and all the world. Right now, in worship, God gives us a taste of His healing, a down payment on our eternal treasure.

So I think the church needs to be more sensitive to the hurting persons of the local congregation. I think the church needs to provide space within its worship for healing. It could be in songs, prayers, preaching, communion, or in a special act of anointing for healing. However a local church chooses to reach out to hurting people, a move in that direction is imperative.

DEVOTIONAL TEACHING

This book on worship would be incomplete without showing the relationship of worship to spiritual growth and development. To grow spiritually means to mature in Christ. Since worship enacts the story of salvation and focuses on Christ who overthrows the powers of evil in the world and in us, a discussion of how worship accomplishes this death to sin and resurrection to life within us is a must.

BIBLICAL BACKGROUND

The Israelites gradually came to see that the covenant they entered into with God (see Exod. 19—24) was a relationship that offered them great familiarity with God and spiritual growth. God was the God of creation and battles, but God also spoke of Himself as Israel's Father, and as a Husband who had taken Israel to Himself in an unending love. In spite of Israel's infidelities through the centuries, God continued to love and care for His people.

The Israelites recognized God's nearness to them and perceived God's "dwelling" with them. God appeared to them at Mount Sinai; was present in the ark and made His abode in the Holy of Holies. In the New Testament, God's nearness took on a new quality in His personalization in Jesus Christ. In Christ, the Godhead actually became a Person and lived in the community of man as part of that fellowship. In Christ a new creation began. The church is the expression of that new life, and to the church Christ promised the gift of the Holy Spirit.

In John 14, Jesus told His disciples He was to go away but that He would not leave them desolate, promising to send the Holy Spirit: "But the Counselor, the Holy Spirit, whom the Father will send in my name, will teach you all things and will remind you of everything I have said to you" (John 14:26).

THE MISSION OF THE SPIRIT

In the above verse we are introduced to the mission of the Spirit. By sending the Spirit to those who believe in Him, Christ desires to share with us the unity He has with the Father. Thus, through faith we are united with the Father, the Son, and the Holy Spirit; we enter into the communion of the Godhead! This communal relationship was accomplished at Pentecost and recognized by Peter as a fulfillment of the Old Testament prophecy of Joel: "Then you will know that I am in Israel that I am the Lord your God and that there is no other . . ." (Joel 2:27, see also vv. 28-29 and Acts 2:17-21).

It is in the church and in its worship where the Holy Spirit especially dwells. The Spirit enters into organic union with each Christian who becomes the "temple" of the Holy Spirit ("Do you not know that your body is a temple of the Holy Spirit, who is in you, whom you have received from God? You are not your own;" [1 Cor. 6:19]). Because of this indwelling, the church as a whole becomes the temple of the Holy Spirit ("In him the whole building is joined together and rises to become a holy temple in the Lord. And in him you too are being built together to become a dwelling in which God lives by his Spirit" [Eph. 2:21-22]).

THE HOLY SPIRIT ENLIVENS OUR UNION WITH CHRIST

It is in the context of the church at worship then, that spiritual growth is to take place. Spiritual growth is not merely accumulating knowledge or adopting a moralistic set of rules; it is the process of becoming adept at communing with God the Father through Jesus Christ by the Holy Spirit.

It is the special role of the Holy Spirit to enable our growth. Whereas our Lord Jesus Christ is the mediator between God and humanity, the Holy Spirit is the communicator between God and humanity. The Holy Spirit communicates God to man and man to God as Paul stated: "Because you are sons, God sent the Spirit of his Son into our hearts, the Spirit who calls out, 'Abba, Father.' So you are no longer a slave, but a son; and since you are a son, God has made you also an heir" (Gal. 4:6-7). This passage speaks to us of the power of the Spirit who works in the very heart of the Christian, transforming him or her into the image of Christ (see Rom. 12:2).

Specifically the work of the Holy Spirit is to communicate within us a transforming power that will reshape our whole lives. It is not just a matter of thinking differently (it is that too), but a matter of living differently. The Bible makes it very clear that we are not to exhibit works of the flesh (see Gal. 5:19-21) but fruits of the Spirit. This fruit is a description of a life-style. It presupposes that "Those who belong to Christ Jesus have crucified the sinful nature with its passions and desires" (Gal. 5:24) and have chosen to display "love, joy, peace, patience, kindness, goodness, faithfulness, gentleness and self-control . . ." (Gal. 5:22-23). In this respect the Holy Spirit's function is to mold both within and without the life of the believer who is growing into union with God. The historical and social context in which this occurs is in the church, which, by the providence of God, has been called to be the new community in a world of broken relationships.

COMMUNICATING GROWTH WITHIN THE WORSHIP OF THE CHURCH

Because growth takes place in the context of community rather than in isolation, the communal nature of Christian learning needs to be recognized. We will look then at the process of learning, which takes place in the Christian community as worship communicates the meaning of the Christian faith and the experience of the Christian life.

COMMUNICATING THE MEANING OF THE CHRISTIAN FAITH THROUGH WORSHIP

An interesting question is raised in Deuteronomy 6. It appears that God is raising the question in Moses' mind. The situation is this: God foresees the descendants of the Israelites raising doubts about the meaning and significance of the religious character of the nation. So God says,

> In the future, when your son asks you, "What is the meaning of the stipulations, decrees and laws the Lord our God has commanded you?" tell him: "We were slaves of Pharaoh in Egypt, but the Lord brought us out of Egypt with a mighty hand. Before our eyes the Lord sent miraculous signs and wonders — great and terrible — upon Egypt and

Pharaoh and his whole household. But he brought us out from there to bring us in and give us the land that he promised on oath to our forefathers. The Lord commanded us to obey all these decrees and to fear the Lord our God, so that we might always prosper and be kept alive, as is the case today. And if we are careful to obey all this law before the Lord our God, as he has commanded us, that will be our righteousness." (Deut. 6:20-25)

The answer God gave the Israelite fathers was to recount Israel's pilgrimage from Egypt through the wilderness and into the Promised Land. Because God is a God who works in history and within a social context, God is revealed through the events of life, particularly those that belong to the people of God. These events are rehearsed in worship.

If we are to be shaped by the Christian faith, we must recover an ability to recite what God has done in history. This includes the Exodus Event and the life of Israel, the Incarnation event, and the life of the early church. In worship we enact the events of God's saving deeds which by the power of the Holy Spirit give shape to our spirituality.

COMMUNICATING THE EXPERIENCE OF THE CHRISTIAN FAITH THROUGH WORSHIP

If it is the meaning of the Christian faith and not just knowledge about the faith that we wish to communicate, then we must ask how that meaning is conveyed. An interesting hint is given to us in Deuteronomy 6 in the instruction God gave to Moses.

These commandments that I give you today are to be upon your hearts. Impress them on your children. Talk about them when you sit at home and when you walk along the road, when you lie down and when you get up. Tie them as symbols on your hands and bind them on your foreheads. Write them on the doorframes of your houses and on your gates. (Deut. 6:6-9)

It is clear from an examination of these words that the emphasis falls on experiencing truth in the context of life. That truth, which is in the heart, must be there when you sit, walk, lie down, and rise. Truth is to be everywhere in the context of living—on your hand, on your forehead, on the doorposts of your house, and on the gates. The point is that the meaning of truth is realized through the experience of truth. Truth is confirmed by the doing of truth.

If the worshiping church is the new humanity and, therefore, the context in which growth is to occur, it is the responsibility of the church to provide the atmosphere in which the Christian faith is made real through experience. The question then with which we have to deal is this: what spiritual means does the church have at its disposal for communicating the experience of faith and thereby fostering growth in its members?

The answer to this question lies in the worship of the church. In worship, the church reenacts the events from which it derives its meaning. Those historical events that give meaning to the church are repeated over and over again; and through them, by the power of the Holy Spirit, the experience of the Christian faith is handed down.

From a theological standpoint it looks like this: God sent His eternal Son, the Word, who became flesh in the Person of Jesus Christ. Jesus communicated the Father by His physical presence, His speaking, and His life, death, and resurrection. Christ, in turn, instructed His church to communicate Himself by its life—by the word it speaks, the life it lives, the hope it bears. This is the job He sent the Holy Spirit to empower us to do. Therefore, as the church reenacts the life of Christ, it communicates Christ. For Christ is not absent from the church, but is present in the church. In this sense worship hands down Jesus Christ. Worship is the context in which Jesus Christ is continually communicated to the believer.

Worship transfers events through recitation and rehearsal. The service of the Word, which consists of reading Scripture and preaching, is an oral recitation of those past events that continue to give meaning to our lives today. A good communicator in reading and preaching is one who can make the events of the past come alive. Preaching re-creates the event and brings it to us by the power of speech. The Holy Spirit works through that proclamation in such a way that the hearer experiences the original event and therefore responds to it in a way similar to those who were actual witnesses.

In the same way the service of the Lord's Supper rehearses the main event of the Christian faith. The elements of bread and wine, the Table of the Lord, the words of institution, the blessing, the breaking, the giving, and the receiving are all part of the enactment through which a real and substantial communication occurs.

Participation in worship is not meant to be rote or casual. It requires an active I'm-really-there-with-Christ approach. It is something the church does, not something the church observes.

The meaning of what is happening is, of course, rooted in the actual historical event. But the experience of that meaningful event is now being re-created in the worship of the church. By going through worship in faith, the believer is using his or her mind, body, emotions, and senses to remember and to give thanks. At the same time his or her senses are opened to God's grace. A two-way communication occurs between the worshiper and God.

For example, baptism, an occasion when a child or an adult is brought into the Christian community, creates an opportunity for the whole congregation to renew their initial commitment to Christ.

Because baptism is the passageway into the church, every baptism is a reminder of each believer's own baptism. In the ancient church it became customary for the whole body to prepare for baptism with the initiates. The baptized believer did not go through the entire preparation but participated in some of the final preparations, particularly the final fastings and the all-night vigil (in the case of Easter baptisms). The vigil consisted of a series of Scripture readings that recount the creation and re-creation of the world and salvation through Christ. Then, when the convert was baptized into Christ and the church, the whole Christian community repeated their baptismal vows to signify their own recommitment to Christ and His church.

In today's church, baptism is too often something we watch. There is a great need to return to baptism as a means not only of bringing new people into the church but of restoring our relationship to God through the communication of the meaning of baptism for everyone in the community.

A second example may be taken from confirmation. In the ancient church, confirmation or Chrism (from the Greek *charis*, meaning "gift" or "grace") was the rite of receiving the Holy Spirit.

Originally the rite was performed immediately after baptism. In the course of time, however, due partially to the practice of infant baptism, confirmation was separated from baptism and became a rite administered in early adulthood.

In Protestant churches today we observe a similar practice. The Baptists dedicate their children and later put them through a period of instruction followed by baptism. The Presbyterians baptize their children and later teach them the catechism, which is then followed by full membership in the church. Even the Wesleyan and Pentecostal belief in a second blessing reminds one of the ancient church practice. Of course, the call to rededication within the fundamentalist and evangelical groups draws on the same tradition.

The point is that maturation in Christ is not only a matter of steady growth but also one of dramatic turning points. There are times when we encounter God in unusual ways. These times ought not to be isolated from the church but be a very part of worship so that our growth occurs in the context of the living community of believers.

Traditionally, confirmation (or the reception of the Holy Spirit) was attended by three signs: the laying on of hands, an anointing of oil, and a signing on the forehead with the sign of the cross.

The laying on of hands is an ancient symbol which originated in the Old Testament, was used by Jesus, and was employed by the apostles to signify the conferral of a blessing.

The anointing with oil signified the giving of the Spirit. The external sign points to the inner anointing of the Spirit. (This is sometimes put so strongly that the Spirit Himself is described as the anointing.) The anointing with oil specifically emphasized the bestowal of the gift of the Spirit.

The signing of the cross on the forehead symbolized dedication to Christ. It pointed to a person's identity with Christ as a soldier who is branded for duty. It was similar to the formalizing of a contract. These symbols when taken seriously were powerful incentives to spiritual growth.

A third example of how worship stimulates our spiritual growth comes from confession. If faith is a matter of hearing the Word of God in such a way that it produces awareness of God (and His claim on our life and the life of the world) and obedience to what we have heard, then there must be an opportunity in the Christian life for the ongoing application of the Word to one's life. It is in the practice of confession where spiritual scrutiny (attended by a turning away from sin and turning toward God) fosters growth in Christ.

Christian psychology recognizes the need for confession in personal growth. Confession is part of the process of redemption, a response-forming process that helps a person act out the goal of a Christian life-style. For this reason confession ought to be accompanied by an expiation that allows the believer not only to turn from sin but also to turn toward a new life in Christ.

Professor Hobart Mowrer explains the significance of expiation this way:

> People do not merely talk themselves into sin; they act. And by the same token, I do not believe anyone ever talks himself out of sin. Again there must be action, and this action must involve not only confession, of an ultimately open type, but also an atonement. Confession without a sober program of expiation can be dangerous, in the sense of causing the individual to be overwhelmed with guilt and self-hatred.

(HERBERT MOWRER, *LEARNING THEORY AND PERSONALITY DYNAMICS*, P. 601)

In the history of the Christian church there are two kinds of confession: public and private. The Reformation churches have incorporated into their worship a form of public confession. It is usually a brief statement, recognizing sin and confessing it to the Lord followed by a statement recognizing the forgiveness of sin provided by God through Jesus Christ. However, public confession is general and does not offer an opportunity to reflect on actual personal sins. In other words, there is not a real grappling with sin in one's own life in public confession. Therefore, perhaps we need to reinstate some form of private confession.

I believe there is a crying need to restore a pastoral concern for the "cure of souls." Pastoral care is not the exclusive responsibility of the minister. The renewal movements in our day, particularly the charismatic renewal, have given the gift of "hearing a confession" back to the congregation. The gift of prescribing a course of action to help a person actualize the life of Christ belongs to the whole church.

If we are concerned to communicate growth in Christ, then we ought to consider a return to private confession as a way of dealing with guilt and releasing persons to continued growth in

Christian character.

Professor Emeritus of pastoral ministries at Asbury Seminary, Curry Mavis, says:

> Guilt feelings are debilitating because they cause one to look backward instead of forward. In doing this they obscure objectives with a loss of motivation . . . Furthermore, guilt feelings are spiritually disabling because they produce anxiety. Anxiety is a psychic and spiritual crippler, as paralysis is to the body. It destroys initiative through a morbid fear of failure. Because guilt holds a person back from growth, there is a need for forgiveness. In forgiveness God redirects our energies and turns a self-destructive, guilt-ridden person into a constructive person whose energies may now be channeled toward becoming a new person in Christ. (*The Psychology of Christian Experience*, p. 27)

I have not attempted to provide an exhaustive list of those activities within the Christian community that stimulate growth. Much needs to be said about the ministries God gives to each of us in the body. We are all called to be ministers to each other, to employ our gifts within the body for the building up of each other. It should be the concern of each worshiping community to provide a free atmosphere in which persons are able to both offer their gifts and receive the gifts of others. When a Christian community expects the minister to be the only minister, it is doomed to fail. Growth occurs through doing; and when those who can minister in the body are ministering, the transformation of life in the context of the body is maximized.

CHALLENGE

The challenge in this chapter is for us to recognize how worship grows individual Christians and nurtures the corporate body.

The heart of worship is the gospel—the good news of God in Jesus Christ. In worship we proclaim, remember, enact, and celebrate the gospel. In doing so, the Christian and the entire worshiping community rehearse both the meaning and the experience of the gospel. This continual rehearsal of the gospel forms us and shapes us into the image of Christ and into the lifestyle characterized by the pattern of death to sin and resurrection to a new life in Christ, a pattern of life empowered by the Spirit.

EPILOGUE

Twila and I have written this book with some specific goals in mind. We are both part of the worship renewal that is happening around the world, and we are both committed to facilitate this renewal in the hearts of believers and in the local church.

In This Sanctuary has not been a "how to" book but a book much more given to reflection on the nature of biblical worship. We both believe this is the place to start in worship renewal because so little seems to be known about the real nature of worship from a biblical view. Far too many churches are running to market-driven, entertainment-oriented worship, which, appealing as it may be, is not rooted in a comprehensive vision of scriptural worship.

So what do we want you to have accomplished or to do as a result of reading and, hopefully, studying this book?

First, we hope that we have made your biblical understanding of worship more complete. Throughout this work we have stressed how the nature of worship is grounded in the story of redemption, the story that connects Genesis to Revelation, Creation to the new heaven and the new earth. In worship we remember, proclaim, enact, and celebrate God's saving deeds, glorifying God through Jesus Christ in the power of the Spirit. We hope that this biblical understanding of worship gives you new insights.

Second, we hope the biblical understanding of worship will enrich your experience of worship. If worship remembers, enacts, proclaims, and celebrates the gospel story, then we as individuals and the corporate body of Christ rehearse our relationship to God in worship. Through that rehearsal we become continually formed and shaped into the pattern of dying to sin and rising to Christ, which is the pattern of His death and resurrection and the pattern of our spirituality.

Third, we hope this book strengthens your role as a leader in worship renewal. We face a crisis in worship renewal today, a crisis between two ways of worship: (1) the restoration of a biblically-driven worship renewal or (2) a pop culture, market-driven approach to worship. We hope that you, as a reader of this book, will think deeply about these alternatives and choose to commit your life and leadership to a renewal in worship that will restore the biblical tradition in a way that is wholly relevant to our contemporary world. Perhaps you could become a student of worship and ultimately a teacher of worship in the local church.

Finally, we recognize that we have only scratched the surface of worship and worship renewal in this book. There is much that we have not covered. Certainly much more needs to be said about the actual practice of worship. How do you take the basic principles and insights we have presented and put them into motion in the local church and in the lives of believers? Because these matters are beyond the scope of this book, we hope you will make worship a lifelong study and a continuing experience of spiritual enrichment.

TWILA PARIS DISCOGRAPHY

1981   *Knowing You're Around* (Benson)
Produced by Wayne Boosahda and Ken Sarkey

1982   *Keeping My Eyes On You* (Benson)
Produced by Jonathan David Brown

1984   *The Warrior Is A Child* (Benson)
Produced by Jonathan David Brown

1985   *Kingdom Seekers* (Star Song)
Produced by Jonathan David Brown

1987   *Same Girl* (Star Song)
Produced by Jonathan David Brown

1988   *For Every Heart* (Star Song)
Produced by Jonathan David Brown

1989   *It's The Thought* (Star Song)
Produced by Jonathan David Brown

1990   *Cry For The Desert* (Star Song)
Produced by Brown Bannister

1991   *Sanctuary* (Star Song)
Produced by Richard Souther

1992   *A Heart That Knows You* (Star Song)
Produced by Greg Nelson, Paul Mills,
Brown Banniser & Jonathan David Brown

1993   *Beyond A Dream* (Star Song)
Produced by Brown Bannister & Paul Mills

ROBERT WEBBER WORSHIP RESOURCES

BOOKS

WORSHIP OLD AND NEW: A BIBLICAL HISTORICAL AND PRACTICAL INTRODUCTION (Grand Rapids: Zondervan, 1994). 2nd Edition. This work, originally published in 1982, is a standard textbook in the field of worship introducing students to the academic study of worship. It summarizes the biblical data, develops a biblical theology of worship, traces the development of worship through the centuries, and presents a study of the practice of worship.

WORSHIP WORKSHOP (Grand Rapids: Zondervan, 1988). This brief work, containing thirteen chapters for an adult study group, addresses worship in the heart, in the home, in the church, and in the world.

WORSHIP IS A VERB (Nashville: Abbott Martyn, 1992). 2nd Edition. This work, originally published by Word in 1985, is directed toward the minister, worship leader, and the worship committee. It is a popular work presenting eight principles that will help make worship participatory. Each of the nine chapters ends with a useful study guide that can be used by Sunday school groups or other small groups.

SIGNS OF WONDER (Nashville: Abbott Martyn, 1992). This popularly-written book addresses the current renewal in worship and introduces the reader to the phenomena of the convergence of traditional and contemporary worship. It contains specific instruction and examples of how to introduce traditional worship into a contemporary worshiping community and how to introduce contemporary worship into a traditional worshiping community.

LITURGICAL EVANGELISM: WORSHIP AS OUTREACH AND NURTURE
(Harrisburg: Morehouse Publishing, 1992). This brief book
is a study of evangelism in the third century with application
to the contemporary church. It investigates the seven steps of
evangelism, all of which occurred in worship, and makes
suggestions on how evangelism and worship may work
together in the contemporary church.

PEOPLE OF THE TRUTH: A CHALLENGE OF THE CHURCH TO
CONTEMPORARY CULTURE (Harrisburg: Morehouse, 1993),
with Rodney Clapp. This work addresses the problems of
contemporary culture and shows how the church as a
community of worship shapes a new society of people.
Because worship enacts the vision of a new people, the
people of worship are shaped into a people who live in
society with a new set of values.

EVANGELICALS ON THE CANTERBURY TRAIL: WHY EVANGELICALS
ARE ATTRACTED TO THE LITURGICAL CHURCH (Harrisburg:
Morehouse Publishing, 1985).

THE BOOK OF DAILY PRAYER (Grand Rapids: Eerdmans, 1993).
This unique devotional book contains Scripture devotions for
every day of the year based on the Christian year. The
readings will organize a spiritual journey around Advent,
Christmas, Epiphany, Lent, Holy Week, Easter, and
Pentecost. Each reading engages the heart, the mind, and the
will and orders experiences into the life of Christ.

THE ALLELUIA! SERIES (Nashville: Abbott Martyn, 1994). Available September, 1994. The ALLELUIA! Series is an inspiring and challenging set of adult books from the Personal Enrichment in Worship Studies Program of the Institute for Worship Studies.

Each stimulating book, designed for the adult study curriculum of the local church, consists of thirteen challenging sessions of study built around: 1) an informative reading; 2) a personal and devotional one-hour assignment to do at home; and 3) a one-hour sharing, open group discussion time for Sunday school or a home study group.

Each study presents the biblical foundations of Christian worship, examples and illustrations from the history of worship, and practical application for immediate personal and corporate worship.

A Certificate of Worship Studies is offered to each student who completes the program.

COURSE AND BOOK TITLES

LEARNING TO WORSHIP WITH ALL YOUR HEART - A study in the biblical foundations of worship.

REDISCOVERING THE MISSING JEWEL - A study in worship through the centuries.

MAKING SUNDAY COME ALIVE! - A study in the services of the Christian year.

SING A NEW SONG! - A study of the role of music and the arts in worship.

REDISCOVERING THE CHRISTIAN FEASTS - A study in the services of the Christian year.

ENCOUNTERING THE HEALING POWER OF GOD - A study in the sacred actions of worship.

EMPOWERED BY THE HOLY SPIRIT - A study in the ministries of worship.

THE COMPLETE LIBRARY OF CHRISTIAN WORSHIP, edited by Robert Webber. (Nashville: Abbott Martyn, 1993, 7 vols.).

This seven-volume work is an indispensable resource for worship and worship renewal.

The first two volumes deal with the more theoretical material, presenting the biblical foundation of worship, historical models of worship, and the church's theological thinking on worship.

Volumes III through VII are more practical in nature and show how the biblical and historical material relate to planning and leading worship, as well as the role of music and the arts in worship. These volumes also provide orders for all the services of the Christian year, as well as orders for the sacred actions of worship and instruction on how worship relates to evangelism, pastoral care, social action, education, work, spiritual formation, and children.

Every major denomination and Christian movement is represented — Orthodox, Catholic, mainline Protestant, Evangelical, Holiness, Pentecostal, and Charismatic.

And no subject has been omitted. You will learn from every tradition. You and your congregation will find innumerable resources and ideas for every occasion of worship.

Volume I The Biblical Foundations of Christian Worship

Volume II The Twenty Centuries of Christian Worship

Volume III The Renewal of Sunday Worship

Volume IV The Role of Music and Arts in Worship

Volume V Services of the Christian Year

Volume VI The Sacred Actions of Worship

Volume VII The Ministries of Worship

THE INSTITUTE FOR WORSHIP STUDIES,
Robert Webber, Director.

The Institute for Worship Studies (IWS) provides worship training for pastors, music ministers, church leaders, and laypeople through academically respectable and highly applicable courses of study.

IWS courses are prepared with the conviction that contemporary worship should be grounded in the Scriptures, draw on the rich treasuries of the church's worship throughout history, and be committed to minister to the needs of the contemporary worshiper.

Consequently, IWS courses teach that the content of Christian worship is the gospel of Jesus Christ which is recalled and enacted when the church gathers to hear God speak and to give thanks at God's Table. IWS courses advocate the creative uses of the arts in worship, call for an evangelical practice of the Christian year, support revitalized sacred actions of worship, and explore ways in which worship empowers the outreach ministries of the church such as evangelism, pastoral care, and social justice.

In addition, IWS courses acknowledge the many styles in which Christian worship takes place—liturgical, traditional, Protestant, free church, creative, charismatic, and convergence. Consequently, IWS courses are prepared in such a way that they serve the worshiper and worship leader of each style of worship. In this way IWS seeks to fulfill its mission to promote a renewal of worship and a renewal of God's people in worship through local churches of all denominations and Christian fellowships.

The Institute for Worship Studies courses of instruction are brought to the student in a home study program. Students do not have to travel to a campus to study. Assignments are all contained in the course text and in the course workbook which guides the student's study step by step.

Because educational specialists recognize that learning is a social activity, the Institute for Worship Studies strongly recommends courses be taken in a group setting wherever possible.

The Institute for Worship Studies offers three Programs of Study:

1) The Layperson's Curriculum. Two different kinds of worship curriculum are made available for the laypeople of the local church. First the Alleluia! worship curriculum

presents seven inspiring, informative, and challenging courses designed for individual study and group discussion. Second, the Worship Teacher's curriculum consists of six courses designed for retreat or classroom study. These courses are for teachers of worship and include full directions and easily accessible materials for both teacher and student.

2) The Worship Leader's Program. This twenty-course program of studies is designed exclusively for those who are leaders of worship in the local church or teachers of worship in undergraduate or graduate settings. Each course is worth three Continuing Education Units (CEU). Take any twelve courses for the worship leader's Diploma in Worship Studies (DWS).

3) The Academic Program. This eight-course program of studies is designed for those who wish to study the biblical roots, the historical development, and the theological understanding of worship. Each of these seminary-level courses is worth four Continuing Education Units (CEU). Take any six courses for an Academic Diploma in Worship Studies (ADWS).

4) The Seminary Credit Program. This seven-course program of studies is designed for students who desire seminary or graduate credit. The courses, which are designed by IWS, are offered through partnership schools for academic credit in programs of study leading to the M.A., M.Div, or D.Min degrees.

For more information about the IWS write:
The Institute for Worship Studies
Post Office Box 894
Wheaton, Illinois 60189-0894